Endorsements

Randy White has an engaging writing style. His commitment to the text of Scripture is refreshing. His interpretation of the text is compelling. Drawing from all of Scripture (beginning with Genesis 1-11), he traces the prophecies of the coming antichrist through the whole of biblical and human history. He speaks with certainty where Scripture is clear; he exercises caution when Scripture is less clear. The consummation of this present age will come. Satan will seek to thwart the purposes of God. The antichrist will deceive the nations. But, the righteous reign of our Redeemer will triumph. This is White's message. This is a riveting read!

Morris H. Chapman,
President and Chief Executive Officer
Executive Committee of the Southern Baptist
Convention

As our world continues on its course toward Armageddon surely the Bible has something to say regarding the unfolding of events. Among the players that stand on center stage in this coming drama is the Antichrist himself. In this volume Randy White pulls back the curtain in hopes of helping us all recognize this world figure for who he is and for what he will do. He writes from a background of Biblical integrity as he brings the issue into view. Read it and reap.

O.S. Hawkins
President and Chief Executive Officer
Guidestone Financial Resources of the Southern
Baptist Convention

Pastor Randy White's investigation of the Antichrist approaches the question of the "man of sin" with care and caution, avoiding many of the pitfalls of sensationalized views often endorsed by careless teachers. At the same time he presents a credible account of the coming of the desperate leader of the final rebellion against God. Everyone will not agree with every detail of his exegesis, but any pastor preaching or teaching on prophetic themes ought to read this book.

Paige Patterson
President
Southwestern Baptist Theological Seminary

Table of Contents

Preface

Someday soon the day is coming.

In just the twinkling of an eye, the world will change dramatically. Unable to discern what has taken place, the talking heads of the newsroom, the power heads of world governments, and the sore-heads at the local coffee shop will begin to make conclusions based on the scenario at hand.

The scenario is that large segments of the population of the Western world have mysteriously disappeared, along with sprinklings of the populations of all nations. Planes have crashed, key leaders are missing, panic has settled in. Newspapers, Internet sites, and Facebook pages will be dominated by the strange, worldwide phenomenon. Twitter will have trending topics such as "disappearance," "rapture," and a few oddball suggestions like "aliens" and "conspiracy."

Through a few days of panic, someone will come up with a plausible answer. Perhaps it was abduction from space aliens or a secret government experiment gone awry. Maybe it was a new, mysterious organism that caused simultaneous combustion within its carriers, leaving no trace behind.

It is the day of the rapture. The Lord Jesus Christ will descend, the angel will sound the trumpet, and believers in Jesus Christ will be snatched up, meeting Jesus in the air. Departing to heaven, all the believers who are alive on this day, along with the believers who died since the resurrection of Jesus, will begin a great reunion of the entire church family, a worship service and celebration in one, falling at Jesus' feet and rejoicing in the marriage supper of the Lamb, preparing ourselves for the triumphant return of

Jesus Christ to this Earth to begin the long-awaited kingdom of God.

Back on Earth, life will slowly but surely begin to return to order. Perhaps immediately, but more than likely a period of several years will pass, perhaps up to thirty years, before the final clock begins its countdown to destruction. That final countdown clock is set with precisely seven remaining years from the time it begins ticking.

During this seven-year period, which we call "the tribulation," the Antichrist will rule and reign—first over a small country, then a growing coalition, and finally over the entire Earth.

Who the Antichrist will be and what he will do has been a matter of speculation and study for two thousand years. Perhaps more speculation than study, but the topic is one of unique interest for almost all of humanity.

- Is he alive today?
- Is he a he, she, it, or they?

- Is he human?
- When can a person know the identity of the Antichrist?

This book attempts to answer all of these questions and more, prayerfully doing so with more study than speculation. Along the journey, take your Bible, use your mind, and be blessed as you come to an understanding of the one the Bible calls "the man of sin."

Someday soon the day is coming!

Chapter 1

How the End Will Come

To understand the identity and role of the Antichrist, you will need to understand eschatology, or end-times theology.

Through the ages Christians have divided themselves into three theological camps that are three distinct worldviews about the world's end.

The postmillennial camp believes that the Antichrist has come and gone. Some would identify him as Tiglath-Pilesar II, Alexander the Great, Nero, or even Hitler. Those in this camp believe that we live (or soon will) in the days in which "Christ's great kingdom will come on earth"[1] and that for a figurative thousand- year period life will get better and better until Jesus comes. While this worldview was popular a hundred years ago, two world wars and history's bloodiest century on record have left few today who hold to this view. The daily paper just doesn't give evidence of a world getting better and better, and scriptural evidence is equally thin. There is, however, a version of postmillennialism popular today among charismatic Christians, and even a growing group of culturally conservative activists, called "dominion," "restoration," or "kingdom now" theology. One of these, Gary DeMar, teaches "Christian Reconstruction" with the understanding that Christ's millennial kingdom will be brought about as we restore biblical Christianity to our nation and around the world. Rather than a world that gets worse and worse, he sees a world that will get better and better (though it may first have a cataclysmic failure that will cause the world to turn to the Christian right for leadership). It is even possible that we will see the rise of politicians (both in America and Israel) who seek to usher in the Messianic Age through legislated morality.

The amillenial camp does not believe in a literal Antichrist. Any teaching of the Antichrist in the Old and New Testaments speaks figuratively of the world's wicked leaders or even of wickedness in general. This camp does not hold to a literal seven-year tribulation, rapture, or millennial kingdom (using standard definitions held for each). Spiritualizing much of the Old and New Testaments, this group believes that in the future there will be one single return of Jesus, who will then consummate the eternal age. Amillenialists are found in almost every seminary of the land, in many of the pulpits, and throughout the world. Some amillenialists are "preterists," those who believe that much, if not all, of the book of Revelation is a description of events which have already passed. Other amillenialists simply view the teachings about end times as figurative and not literal language.

Only the premillennial camp believes in a literal Antichrist who is yet to come. Only the premillennial camp consistently interprets the Old and New Testaments literally in matters of end times. Only the premillennial camp (and only one segment of that camp!) believes in a coming rapture, followed by a tribulation in which the Antichrist will reign.

I am an unapologetic premillennialist. I came to this conviction after great study to "rightfully divide the word of truth," as instructed in 2 Timothy 2:15. Believing that God is the author of the Bible, that He said what He meant and meant what He said, that He was speaking *objectively* and that we cannot therefore interpret His words *subjectively*, I concluded that a premillennial theological perspective of world events is most biblical.

With this conviction I have taken every prophetic word about the Antichrist and tried to come up with the best possible scenario for a literal outcome. I pray that each of the teachings of this book has a strong basis from the Scripture. While one may reject my interpretation, I pray that none will reject the literal nature of God's Word.

How to Spot an Amillennialist

As I mentioned before, amillennialists are found in almost every seminary and in many of pulpits. You should know that when you have stumbled upon an amillennialist, you have found someone who is willing to take at least some degree of liberty in interpreting Scriptures that, it would seem, were written with a literalist interpretation in mind. That amillennialists do not take Scripture literally can be seen in several facets:

- They deny or redefine Christ's millennial reign on earth, though it is graphically described in the Old Testament prophets and clearly taught in Revelation 20:1-10.
- They spiritualize key prophetic Scriptures of both the Old and New Testaments. Terms like "1,000 years" mean "a long time," and pictures such as "the wolf shall lie down with the lamb" mean "peace, love, and harmony shall finally

prevail." Referring to God's "everlasting covenant" with Israel Genesis 17:7, one spiritualized comment that is typical of amillennialism is, "The word for 'everlasting' is 'olam,' which comes from the root 'to be hidden.' The literal meaning therefore is 'as far as one can see,' or 'unto the dim unknown.'"[2] Such spiritualization does not deny the authority of the text but often changes its most clear meaning.

• They may too quickly dismiss key points of theology. For example, an amillenialist will focus on John the Baptist's "repent" message while overlooking the *reason* for repentance, namely that "the kingdom of heaven is at hand." More commentary will be given to John's fashion faux pas and dining habits than to the central core of his message: The Kingdom of God! Because the Kingdom theology of the Old Testament, when taken literally, does not fit the amillenial perspective, discussion of it is spiritualized or nonexistent.

Many others call themselves "panmillennialists," saying, "It will all pan out in the end!" If we were not instructed to be diligent in searching the Scriptures and rightly dividing them, this would be acceptable, but with the commands of both Testaments, we must go further to find answers to life's questions.

The matters concerning the end times, let alone the journey between now and then, are too great to leave to the spiritualizing and allegorizing techniques of the amillennialists and the instruction to search the Scriptures too comprehensive to ignore the events of the future. The Bible is full of answers to life's dilemmas (past, present, and future) but only when it is properly handled.

If you are an amillennialist, let me help set you on the same path to premillennialism I once traveled. You will find that the Bible will come to life when rightly handled, and answers to questions you once thought unanswerable will become clear right before your eyes.

Journey to Premillennialism

The expedition begins with Genesis 1:1! Every premillennialist takes these inaugural words of our history at face value: "In the beginning God created the heavens and the earth." Can you embrace the reality that God has eternally existed before the beginning, that He created the beginning, and that all the content which makes up our created lives was produced at His Word? Going further, can you accept one of the first revelations of the Bible, namely that man and woman were created in the image of God, that they were created complete, intelligent, fully developed, and fully human? Can you then accept the teaching that God commanded the first man, Adam, to cultivate the garden in which he was placed and to eat from its trees all he wanted with the exclusion of one tree, the tree of knowledge of good and evil? Do you take literally the reality that Adam and Eve rejected this prohibition and partook of that fruit, and death then came into the world, together with many other adverse effects in what we call "the fall"?

If you are with me so far, you are well on your way to premillennialism!

In Genesis 3:15, in conjunction with the fall, is one of the indispensable verses of the Old Testament, "And I will put enmity between you and the woman, and between your seed and her seed; he shall bruise you on the head, and you shall bruise him on the heel." This is the first mention of the coming Christ! This prophetic word tells us that Satan will lose the battle with a fatal crushing of the head but that the coming One would only receive a "bruise on the heel." With this word, God set His plan into place to redeem fallen man from his sin and its destruction.

With this Word, God said that the Christ would come through a woman! Now we have our first clue toward the fulfillment of the plan of God.

That woman, Eve, gave birth to two sons, Cain and Abel. When the first was born, she declared, "I have gotten a manchild with the help of the LORD,"

21

and she named the child "Cain," which means "the gotten one." Eve evidently believed that this child was the one God would provide through the seed of a woman who would crush the serpent's head.

Rather than Christ, however, Cain turned out to be Antichrist, not in personage but in type. First John 3:12 says that Cain, "was of the evil one," and of the Antichrist it is said that the devil is his father (John 8:44). Many are the comparisons between Cain and the Antichrist:

- Cain at first appears to be the Promised One, but later his true identity is clear.
- Cain wanted to appear sincere in his religion but was empty in his presentation of sacrifice.
- Cain killed his brother, as the Antichrist later will do to the Jews in the tribulation.
- Cain was a liar ("I don't know where by brother is!"), and the Antichrist will be part of the "deluding influence" upon end-times citi-

zens, "so that they will believe what is false" (2 Thess. 2:11).

- God had the final judgment on Cain as He will for the Antichrist. Cain was "cursed from the ground" (Gen. 4:11), and the Antichrist will be "cast alive into the lake of fire" (Rev. 19:20).[3]

Cain was just the introduction to the foreshadowing of the real Antichrist! While Cain turned out not to be the Christ or the Antichrist (but a model thereof), both the genuine Christ and the real Antichrist were yet to come.

Now, if you have been able to accept Genesis 1–2 (the existence of God and the creation of man), Genesis 3 (the sinful choice of man and the curse that followed, as well as the pledge of a coming Christ), and Genesis 4 (the birth of a son, who was thought to be the Promised One but who turned out to be the exact opposite) as literal, then you, my friend, are well on your way to being a card-carrying premillenialist!

Some in the theological world have not made it this far. They view the record of creation as an artistic expression or theological perspective about origins. They see Adam and Eve as representative of the first human beings and not literally the original humans themselves. They see the partaking of the fruit as a fable that displays the poor choices mankind has made in general, in contrast to deliberate disobedience to God that Adam and Eve made in particular. They understand Genesis 3 to describe, in a poetic way, how these poor choices have consistently made life arduous for each of us. They see Genesis 3:15 as the heart's expression of optimism for better days. In other words, they take it all spiritually or symbolically or allegorically but not literally. The mark of a premillennialist is his or her literal acceptance of all Scriptures that context does not allow to be taken differently.

Coming to the end times, then, the premillennialist reads that believers will be "caught up in the air" almost in unison with the "dead in Christ" rising from their grave (see 1 Thess. 4:13-18). Reading this literally, they see this as teaching "rapture" (Latin for "caught up"). Following their gathering to the Lord in the air, premillennialists understand that the events of the tribulation will begin to unfold on Earth as they are literally taught in Revelation 6–19, Matthew 24, and other Old and New Testament Scriptures. When they read that the devil shall be enchained for one thousand years, they take it as they read it! This is a premillennialist. (More specifically, a pretribulation premillenialist, for there are some, called "historic premillennialists" who believe the rapture will commence the millennium. Pre-tribulation premillenialists often classify themselves as "dispensationalists").

What does a postmillennialist, amillennialist, or panmillennialist do with these teachings? He or she either ignores them (while the premillennialist explores them) or spiritualizes them (while the premillennialist conceptualizes them, seeking to discover ways in which they can be literally realized).

If you take Genesis 1–4 literally, you will have no problem taking great prophetic passages like Daniel, Ezekiel, and Isaiah literally. Each is filled with precise guidance about the end times, including portraits of the Antichrist that are so clear it is almost impossible not to see his image. In addition, you will have no difficulty embracing as literal the end-times teachings of Christ Himself, or of His beloved disciple John, or of the apostle Paul. With this wealth of literal information, the pieces begin to come together for the end time's mystery, including the identity and modus operandi of the Antichrist himself.

So exactly who is the Antichrist?

Chapter 2

His Origin

Even those with barely a casual familiarity of the Antichrist understand that this global tyrant will have a meteoric rise to leadership, coming out of nowhere to develop into the most powerful man in the world. Can such a rise take place?

In the 2008 presidential election, Americans learned how quickly a person can go from unknown to the centers of power and leadership. Barack Obama began the decade as a state senator from Illinois. First elected to the state senate in 1996 in an unopposed race, twelve years later he was accepting the Democratic nomination for President of the United

States. On the Republican side, Sarah Palin was accepting the nomination for Vice President of the United States twelve years after being elected mayor of her hometown of Wasilla, Alaska. Twelve years prior, either candidate was one whom you could look up in the local phone book, meet for lunch about a community issue, or run into as he or she was walking alone down a city sidewalk.

This kind of meteoric rise is not really all that uncommon. It happens regularly in politics, business, science, and entertainment. Wal-Mart seemingly came from nowhere to become the nation's largest retailer. E-bay and Amazon were unheard of just a few years ago. Even more fresh on the scene are names like YouTube, Facebook, and Twitter. One laboratory discovery can bring worldwide publicity to the work of an unknown scientist. Superstars are born in Hollywood overnight. In the sports arena an unknown like Michael Phelps can quickly become one of the most recognized names and faces in the entire world.

Roots in Rome

Daniel 7 holds an enormously important prophecy about the Antichrist. Recorded by the prophet Daniel while he was exiled in Babylon after the fall of Jerusalem in 586 BC, Daniel noted a vision that he could not have understood but that was perfectly fulfilled in the years to come, partially in Daniel's own lifetime.

Perhaps you have heard that you should write down your dreams. After just a few waking moments, the details of our dreams quickly escape our minds. If you are like most of us, it is not just the particulars of your dreams that quickly escape but other details such as the location of your car keys, the time of your appointment, and sometimes even the day of the week!

Fortunately for us Daniel quickly wrote the details of the dream. His dream was of four beasts, one coming after another. The first was lion-like, with eagle's wings. The wings, however, began to be plucked, and the lion was made to stand on two feet like a man, and this beast was given a human mind.

The second beast resembled a bear, raised up on one side, with three ribs clinched in its teeth. The beast was ferocious and was told to "arise, devour much meat!" (Dan. 7:5).

Next Daniel saw a leopard-like beast with four wings and four heads and great dominion. Finally Daniel saw the fourth and final beast.

Unlike any of the others, this beast was much more "dreadful and terrifying and extremely strong; and it had large iron teeth" (Dan. 7:7). This beast had ten horns. Daniel said he was contemplating those horns when "another horn, a little one, came up among them, and three of the first horns were pulled out by the roots before it; and behold, this horn possessed eyes like the eyes of a man and a mouth uttering great boasts." That this horn is the Antichrist we will see soon, but let's back up and review these beasts.

Daniel 7:16 tells us that these four beasts designate four kings and kingdoms. Historical records and good research help us identify these four kingdoms.

Daniel was living in the days of the kingdom of Babylon. Even to this day the Babylonian kingdom is characterized by a lion with eagle's wings. Nebuchadnezzar, its king, was made to live like a beast but then was restored to his sanity, "given the mind of a man," and returned to the throne. The Babylonian Empire, however, fell quickly—even in Daniel's lifetime—to the kingdom of the Medes and the Persians. The bear, raised up higher on one side than the other (the Persians always overshadowed the Medes), was the tool God used to allow the Jews to return to their homeland in the days of Ezra and Nehemiah.

The third beast is only described in one concise verse, but we can conclude that this is the empire of Alexander the Great. Coming in like a leopard, swift and strong, Alexander overtook the known world by the age of thirty-five, and while he had characteristics of the Antichrist, he certainly was not the man. This third beast had four heads, signifying the four-fold division of Alexander's kingdom after his death. More will come of this third kingdom in pages to come when we discuss the identity of the Antichrist.

After the kingdom of Alexander, the Romans eventually rose to dominion. This "beast" was more "dreadful and strong" than any of the other kingdoms. Rome remains to this day the last of the worldwide empires. Often ruthless in its decrees, the Roman Caesar came to see himself as God, thus becoming another foreshadow of the Roman Caesar yet to come—the Antichrist..

We know that as a world empire Rome did not last. However, fragments of Rome are all around us. Our own congress and senate have roots in the Roman senate, as do the parliaments of countries the world over. Not only the political system, but the legal system, architecture, engineering, litera-ture, theater, city planning, and much more of the old Roman Empire still live on. Even a large majority of the words of the English language (not to mention Spanish, Italian, Portuguese, French, Romanian, and more!) have roots in Latin, the official language of the Roman Empire!

Rome lives today through the governments, languages, and customs of most of Europe and the Western world.

The Antichrist has Roman roots!

But what of those ten horns? Daniel was given a clear answer: "As for the ten horns, out of this kingdom [the kingdom of the dreadful beast: Rome] ten kings will arise; and another [this is the one we want to watch!] will arise after them, and he will be different from the previous ones and will subdue three kings" (Dan. 7:24).

Ten kings yet to arise, each coming from the fragments of the old Roman Empire. The rise of ten nations from Roman scraps is not hard to imagine at all with the rise of strong European Community nations. It is not hard to imagine yet another king that will arise and subdue three of the previous. And what of this final king? Daniel goes on to explain: "He will speak out against the Most High and wear down the saints of the Highest One, and he will intend to make alterations in times and in law; and they will be given into his hand for a time, times, and half a time" (Dan. 7:25).

The origins of the Antichrist? It all begins in Rome!

From Kingdom to King

The fourth beast in Daniel's vision is a kingdom, the kingdom of Rome. From this kingdom ten kingdoms will arise, then another, which will begin to have dominion, first over three, eventually over all.

In the Revelation, the apostle John is also given a vision of a beast. His vision, however, is not of a kingdom, but of a king. John's vision is a compilation of Daniel's. John sees only one beast, with the interesting characteristics of a leopard, a bear, and a lion.

This beast had ten horns, and "the whole earth was amazed and followed after the beast" (Rev. 13:3).

Daniel speaks of kingdoms to come, and John speaks of an evil king to come. In Daniel 9:24-27, there is a word about a "Prince to come." Daniel foresaw a day when the "people of the Prince" would destroy the city of Jerusalem. This would take place after the Messiah has been "cut off." In AD 70, just over thirty-five years after the death of Jesus—in the lifetime of John, Paul, and other first-century believers—the city of Jerusalem was destroyed by the Romans. This fact gives us corroborating evidence that our designation of the fourth beast as Rome is correct. If Daniel tells us that "the people of the Prince" are those who will destroy Jerusalem after the Messiah is "cut off," then the Prince must be of the same people as those who destroyed Jerusalem—once again, the Romans.

Daniel says that the horn "was waging war with the saints and overpowering them" (Dan. 7:21), and John says that the Antichrist will "make war with the saints and to overcome them" (Rev. 13:7).

Daniel says, "He will speak out against the Most High" (Dan. 7:25). John says he will have "a mouth speaking arrogant words and blasphemies" (Rev. 13:5).

Daniel says he will rule for "time, times, and half a time," a prophetic rendering of three and one-half years (Dan. 7:25) while John says the Antichrist will have "authority to act for forty-two months" (Rev. 13:5).

Daniel says, "He will put a stop to sacrifice" (Dan. 9:27). Paul says he will "take his seat in the temple of God, displaying himself as being God" (2 Thess. 2:4).

Without a doubt the prophet Daniel has seen the face of the one to come.

A Crisis of Leadership

How does a charismatic personality rise from nowhere to become the world's premier dictator? One word: CHAOS!

After the rapture of the church, the world becomes a place of chaos, much in need of a savior.

Lee Iacocca, himself a superstar product of chaos, has said, "We are continuously faced by great opportunities brilliantly disguised as insoluble problems." The archives of history, both political and economic, are filled with the biographies of those who, in a time of crisis, stepped in and quickly provided robust leadership, setting their name in stone for the ages to come.

The greatest crisis-born leader of the ages will be the Antichrist.

Daniel says that "a despicable person will arise, on whom the honor of kingship has not been conferred, but he will come in a time of tranquility and seize the kingdom by intrigue" (Dan. 11:21). The phrase "he shall come in a time of tranquility" is difficult for translators, often incorrectly conveying that the times are peaceful when he arrives. Rather, Daniel says that he shall be the bearer of peace (tranquility), the one who is "calm, cool, and collected" when chaos is at every turn. When this "smooth, suave, and sophisticate" comes in peace to a world of chaos, the world will quickly welcome him with open arms.

Here is how *The Message* presents the scene:

His place will be taken by a reject, a man spurned and passed over for advancement. He'll surprise everyone, seemingly coming out of nowhere, and will seize the kingdom. He'll come in like a steamroller, flattening the opposition. Even the Prince of the Covenant will be crushed. After negotiating a cease-fire, he'll betray its terms. With a few henchmen, he'll take total control. Arbitrarily and impulsively, he'll invade the richest provinces. He'll surpass all his ancestors, near and distant, in his rape of the country, grabbing and looting, living with his cronies in corrupt and lavish luxury.

Absalom, son of David, came close to winning the kingdom by his suave ways. Second Samuel 14:25 says, "Now in all Israel was no one as handsome as Absalom, so highly praised; from the sole of his foot to the crown of his head there was no defect in him." Mr. Perfect comes along, and what does he do? When someone approached the palace with a problem, Mr. Perfect would meet them at the gate, and with flattery would win them over.

Then Absalom would say to him, "See, your claims are good and right, but no man listens to you on the part of the king." Moreover, Absalom would say, "Oh that one would appoint me judge in the land, then every man who has any suit or cause could come to me and I would give him justice." And when a man came near to prostrate himself before him, he would put out his hand and take hold of him and kiss him. In this manner Absalom dealt with all Israel who came to the king for judgment; so Absalom stole away the hearts of the men of Israel (2 Sam. 15:3-6).

What does this have to do with the Antichrist? He uses the same tactics as Absalom, and like Absalom the Antichrist finds flattery to be completely effective! He will "obtain the kingdom by flatteries" (Dan. 11:21).

John also speaks of the Antichrist's rise to power. John's vision was of a scroll, sealed with seven seals. The breaking of each seal in the opening of the scroll will bring the commencement of a major event in the years of the tribulation. I believe that the scroll is the "title deed" to the earth. God gave control to Adam and Eve in the garden, telling them to "have dominion" over the earth. Adam and Eve lost that control when, by flattery, the serpent took it from them. In the end God will win back that which is His, having redeemed it on the cross of Christ!

Consider John's record of the breaking of the first seal: "Then I saw when the Lamb broke one of the seven seals, and I heard one of the four living creatures saying as with a voice of thunder, 'Come.' I looked, and behold, a white horse, and he who sat on it had a bow; and a crown was given to him, and he went out conquering and to conquer" (Rev. 6:1-2).

With these words John introduces the Antichrist. He comes on a white horse, bearing a bow with no arrow, signifying his "peaceful" objectives. A crown is given to him, and he begins to conquer.

In the midst of chaos, a "savior" comes.

Chapter 3

Does That Star-Spangled Banner Yet Wave?

We've read of Babylon, Persia, Greece, and Rome. We know of the important role of Jerusalem and Israel. But what about the United States of America?

Only by the greatest expanse of ingenuity can you read of the USA in the Bible. Granted, it is not hard to find those with that kind of creativity, but no tenable method of interpreting Scripture finds a specific reference to the United States in the pages of the Bible. The scenarios I give below are, by necessity, nothing but informed speculation.

What happened to the greatest venture into democracy the world has ever known? Surely a nation as large, powerful, and prominent as the United States would have some quality role in the last day's government, wouldn't it?

I believe there are three possibilities concerning the United States. In advance, I must warn you that none of the three gives any hope for our future. As much as I love this country, I find it impossible to believe that the Star-Spangled Banner, as we know it, will continue to be the standard of liberty during the distressful last days of this age. Perhaps, and I pray not, our flag will cease to wave even much sooner than when the tribulation begins.

Loss of Moral Courage

History has shown that most empires die from within before the enemy without comes in to clean up the mess. Before the Northern Kingdom of Israel fell to the Assyrians in 721 BC, prophets had been preaching doom and gloom messages for generations.

When Amos the prophet came to Israel preaching doom and gloom on neighboring nations, all the people said, "Amen!" But when Amos turned his heart toward home, they said, "Oh my!"

For Amos to talk about the greed, idolatry, and vice of the neighbors was fine, but Amos went to meddling when he said to Israel, "I will not revoke its punishment, because they sell the righteous for money and the needy for a pair of sandals," and they "turn aside the way of the humble; and a man and his father resort to the same girl in order to profane My holy name." Further, "on garments taken as pledges they stretch out beside every alter, and in the house of their God they drink the wine of those who have been fined" (Amos 2:6-8). Because of this sin, God would send punishment:

"Flight will perish from the swift,
And the stalwart will not strengthen his power,

Nor the mighty man save his life.

He who grasps the bow will not stand his
    ground,

The swift of foot will not escape,

Nor will he who rides the horse save his life.

Even the bravest among the warriors will flee
    naked in that day," declares the LORD
    (Amos 2:14-16).

To the south, Judah had a slower decay from within and lasted 135 years longer than its northern partner. The storyline, however, was still the same; decline from within followed by the enemy from without. Like the Northern Kingdom, Judah had plenty of prophets to warn of the looming day of doom. Like the Northern Kingdom, Israel spurned the saving message.

Generally the inner decay sets in decades or more before the nation falls. Sometimes the nation remains in name, but the heart of the nation is radically altered. Today's Western Europe has nothing of the heart and spirit for which it was once known. The expansionist passions of Europe (fanned in no small measure by a longing to spread the gospel of Jesus Christ to new lands) that discovered the New World no longer remain though many of the country names and borders live on. The missionary fires of England have been so extinguished that what once fueled the desire to spread the Christian message to unreached lands, and that was at the heart of European prolif-eration for hundreds of years, has now given way to such Christian void that today these same lands are the beneficiaries of Christian missionary activity rather than benefactors.

The United States of America was born in prin-cipled courage. When our pilgrim fathers landed at Jamestown, they celebrated through worship because they had come to worship. Personal freedoms and liberties and the ability to forge their own future were at the heart of their life-threatening quest across the Atlantic to an unknown and uncertain destiny. It took two hundred years for these forefathers to convey their notions of liberty to fulfillment in a nation born of their struggle and to achieve their purpose. These two hundred years, from 1620 to 1820, were overflowing with stories of moral courage.

Has the tide of courage upon which the *Mayflower* sailed begun to ebb?

Today little courage is evident among believers, even among the Christian faithful. Churches are filled with passive members who lack a primary comprehension of biblical values. Today, if a church can get one-third of its members to attend on any given Sunday, it is doing well. Rare is the church that is not on the decline (and in denial!).

Politically, there is much talk but little action. We have voted ourselves a raise over and over, and now we depend on the government sow for our milk. Until recently, when a disaster approached or after it passed, individuals took care of themselves and their possessions. What they could not move, they insured; what they could not insure, they were prepared to lose. Today, when a disaster like a hurricane approaches, we reach to the government to take guardianship of all of us. We have created such welfare cultures and dependent attitudes that we find large segments of the population unable to take care of themselves and expectant that the government will do so. If the government does not handhold its citizens to safety, the media will cry foul. How different this is from 1792, when "We, the people" held the hand of government and kept it in line; we were the parent, and the government was the child. This kind of freedom takes moral courage, to a great extent lost in America today.

Without a return of principled boldness, our future is dim. A return of such boldness, of moral courage, will come only with a spiritual awakening.

Perhaps this is why America is not mentioned in the end times.

Loss of Military Courage

In its finest days America had military bravery that just would not stop. It was in our DNA, spun into the fabric of our national soul.

In the early days General Washington and his troops, encamped in a cold Valley Forge winter—underfed, poorly clothed, ill-equipped—would not let the reality that they were far outnumbered and overpowered diminish their determination to let freedom ring.

In the midst of lost morale and on the edge of giving up, members of Washington's Continental Army received the words of Thomas Paine, words from his essay "The Crisis" that became a key to the success of that early American army: "These are times that try men's souls; the summer soldier and the sunshine patriot will, in this crisis, shrink from the service of his country; but he that stands it now, deserves the love and thanks of man and woman. Tyranny, like hell, is not easily conquered; yet we have this consolation with us, that the harder the conflict, the more glorious the triumph."

On Christmas Day, 1776, just a few days after being inspired by Paine's words, General Washington led twenty-four hundred soldiers across the Delaware River. Each of them knew the password: victory or death.

How far from today's world. With victory in sight, we have been known to retreat. With the relative loss of a few, we are ready to give in. Modern America has such a lack of military courage that this country has lost wars that, militarily, were already won.

We have become a community of summer soldiers.

May God bless those who commit to victory or death. This disposition has seen us from 1776 to this day. Could the loss of this attitude be the reason we are of no mention in the end times?

Decimated by Rapture

One further, and more positive, scenario remains. It is possible, even probable, that the concluding scenario of the rapture is the final straw that breaks the country's back.

When the rapture occurs—and nothing is keeping its occurrence save the mercy and patience of Almighty God—large sections of America will be left decimated. Of all the nations of the world, perhaps the United States will be more negatively affected by the rapture than any other. Sadly, some nations will scarcely notice the rapture.

America, on the other hand, still has a sizable population base of born-again believers. While some areas will stand less affected by a loss of the Christian population, some communities and regions would lose a large share of the population, including key figures in their government and perhaps a greater part of their teachers, first responders, and businessmen and women.

In a recent sampling, 82 percent of those surveyed identified themselves as Christians. While few would contend that these 82 percent have a saving relationship with Jesus Christ, the number is nonetheless large enough to merit an argument for an enormous and rapid breakdown of our national strength following the removal of the born-again community, instantaneously and without notice. Make no mistake, should the USA remain until the day of the rapture, it will develop into a Third-World country in an instant. This country—then ravaged by crime, hunger, lawlessness, and chaos—will long for a "savior" of its own. It is easy to imagine a scenario in which America quickly succumbs to the leadership of anyone who can help.

Even if that person is the Antichirst.

Chapter 4

Jewish by Race

I love the Jews. I believe they are God's elect and will have a central role in both the future tribulation and the following millennial age, in which they will be the preeminent ethnic race. I do not believe the church replaced the Jews nor that the role of the Jews was revoked by their rejection of the Messiah or subsequent actions. The nation of Israel as a Jewish state should be honored and blessed, prayed for and supported.

I say that because some will doubtlessly take my remarks out of context and charge an anti-Semitic sentiment behind these words. I only ask that judgment be based on my firm and steadfast preaching on behalf of and with support for the nation of Israel.

That said, I am persuaded that the Bible teaches that the Antichrist is a Jewish male.

In Ezekiel 21 the prophet delivers an observation about the fate of Jerusalem and its inhabitants. Many interpreters would say that verses 25-27 concern Zedekiah, the last man to sit on the throne of David as a king of Jerusalem. However, several things in these verses point beyond Zedekiah to one yet to come. Let's consider the passage.

"And you, O slain, wicked one, the prince of Israel, whose day has come, in the time of the punishment of the end," thus says the Lord God, "Remove the turban and take off the crown; this *will* no longer *be* the same. Exalt that which is low and abase that which is high. 'A ruin, a ruin, a ruin, I will make it. This also will be no more until He comes

whose right it is, and I will give it *to Him*'"
(Ezek. 21:25-27, italics added).

Ezekiel speaks of . . .

- One who is slain. John speaks of the Antichrist
  as one who was slain (Rev. 13:3).
- One who is vile and wicked. No better words
  could describe this man of sin.
- One who is "the prince of Israel." As we will
  come to see, this is a role the Antichrist will
  fulfill.
- One "whose day has come." Paul tells us that
  the Antichrist is being restrained "so that in his
  time he will be revealed" (2 Thess. 2:6)
- One "whose day" is scheduled for "the time of
  the punishment of the end," clearly a reference
  to a latter-day prince and not a contemporary
  of Ezekiel.

- One who will experience a threefold ruin, possibly a reference to the three-plus years of the wicked portion of the Antichrist's reign.

- One whose authority will be taken from him and given to the One who comes "whose right it is." Jesus Christ is that One, and He will cast the Antichrist into the lake of fire!

While the interim fulfillment of this passage may have been seen in Zedekiah, the full truth is not to be seen until the time of the end. These verses give us a picture of the Antichrist.

But what is the most startling aspect of the picture? He is a "prince of Israel." He is a Jew.

Later in Ezekiel 28 we witness another picture of the Antichrist. This time the Antichrist makes himself to be a god, gains riches for his treasuries, and is the ruler of many. Even so, in verse 10 we read that he "will die the death of the uncircumcised." The implication is that this is unusual and unanticipated.

If he is a circumcised Jew, we would not expect him to "die the death of the uncircumcised."

Moving to Daniel 11:36-37 we see once more this Antichrist, who does as he pleases, postures himself to be God, flourishes for a time, shows no regard for any other god besides himself, and, specifically "will show no regard for the gods of his fathers." Do not let the plural "gods" confuse you. In Hebrew, the term *God* and *gods* are the same word—transliterated *Elohim*. Literally, this verse says, "He will show no regard for Elohim of his fathers."

Did you catch that? The Antichrist shows no regard to Elohim. Which Elohim? The One of his fathers. The Elohim of Abraham, Isaac, and Jacob. The God of the Jews.

Not yet persuaded? Let's move to the New Testament. To establish the foundation, we need to learn a little Greek.

Greek, which is fortunately a precise language, has two words for *another*. The word *heteros* is for "another of a different kind" while *allos* is "another of the same kind." This is important in understanding John 5:43, "I have come in My Father's name, and you do not receive Me; if another comes in his own name, you will receive him."

Jesus says to the Jews that He came to His people, in the name of His Father, but they did not receive Him. If later, Jesus says, another of the same kind (*allos*) will come, then "you will receive him." Jesus was of the Jewish kind with Jewish roots, saying that while He was rejected as Messiah, the one they would receive as the Messiah would be another, but of the same kind: Jewish.

It makes sense. The Antichrist is acceptable by the Jews as their Savior, their Messiah. He will be believed to be, for the first half of his reign, the promised one. No self-respectful Jew would embrace a Gentile Messiah! For every reason imaginable—theological, political, social—the Antichrist must be Jewish.

Jeremy Gimpel and Tobias Singer have a fascinating radio and Internet television show about Jewish issues. Their program is broadcast overlooking the Temple Mount in Jerusalem. The show takes a question-and-answer format. In one edition the question was posed, "What are the Jews looking for in the Messiah?" The answer is revealing. Mr. Gimpel noted that the Messiah is "simply the representation of the Jewish leadership" and thus Jews "are not supposed to be sitting down waiting for some Messiah. . . . On the contrary each individual Jew has an obligation in literally ushering in the Messianic age in his actions." Rabbi Singer continues, "He [the Messiah] is a vessel, he is like David. In every generation there has to be someone standing by ready to sit on the throne of David. From the time of David 2800 years ago...there has always been a descendent of David alive who potentially could have brought the messianic age."[4]

As you can see, this messianic theology opens the door for a false messiah to be welcomed by the people of Israel and Jews around the world.

Is it anti-Semitic speech to speak of a Jewish Antichrist? No more than to speak of Hitler as German, Stalin as Russian, Pol Pot as Cambodian, or Edi Amin as Ugandan. This is just the frankness of Scripture, which I believe will become a truth of history.

What character of Jew will the Antichrist be? Amazingly, we already have a picture of him, a fore-shadow of the Antichrist, in the person of Judas.

It will help to see the heartache of betrayal as an "inside job" if you consider Psalm 55. Read this psalm below with the understanding that it describes the days of the Tribulation. Imagine yourself as a Jew, experiencing the unrelenting persecution of the Tribulation. It is Hitler's holocaust all over again for the Jewish people, and this is your cry:

> Give ear to my prayer, O God;
> And do not hide Yourself from my supplication.
> Give heed to me and answer me;

I am restless in my complaint and am surely
distracted,
Because of the voice of the enemy,
Because of the pressure of the wicked;
For they bring down trouble upon me
And in anger they bear a grudge against me.
My heart is in anguish within me,
And the terrors of death have fallen upon me.
Fear and trembling come upon me,
And horror has overwhelmed me.
I said, "Oh, that I had wings like a dove!
I would fly away and be at rest.
Behold, I would wander far away,
I would lodge in the wilderness.
I would hasten to my place of refuge
From the stormy wind and tempest" (vv. 1-8).

Having given a general cry of anguish, the Jew
now begins to cry about what is happening "in the
city," a reference to Jerusalem.

Confuse, O Lord, divide their tongues,

For I have seen violence and strife in the city.

Day and night they go around her upon her
walls,

And iniquity and mischief are in her midst.

Destruction is in her midst;

Oppression and deceit do not depart from her
streets (vv. 9-11).

Next the psalmist cries that the worst of the tribulation is neither the universal distress nor the devastation of the city of Jerusalem. As bad as these are, the most unbearable aspect of it all is the source of the destruction:

For it is not an enemy who reproaches me,

Then I could bear it;

Nor is it one who hates me who has exalted
himself against me,

Then I could hide myself from him.

But it is you, a man my equal,

My companion and my familiar friend;

We who had sweet fellowship together

Walked in the house of God in the throng

    (vv. 12-14).

Like Judas, the Antichrist is "a man my equal, my companion and my familiar friend." He is one with whom the Jewish nation "had sweet fellowship together" and "walked in the house of God in the throng." Betrayed by a friend, the psalmist takes comfort in the sovereignty of His changeless God:

Let death come deceitfully upon them;

Let them go down alive to Sheol,

For evil is in their dwelling, in their midst.

As for me, I shall call upon God,

And the LORD will save me.

Evening and morning and at noon, I will

    complain and murmur,

And He will hear my voice.

He will redeem my soul in peace from
    the battle which is against me,
For they are many who strive with me.
God will hear and answer them—
Even the one who sits enthroned from
    of old—
With whom there is no change,
And who do not fear God (vv. 15-19).

Now the psalmist turns his attention again to the Antichrist. Notice how closely the words of this psalm describe the actions of the Antichrist as portrayed in other Scriptures:

He has put forth his hands against those who
    were at peace with him;
He has violated his covenant.
His speech was smoother than butter,
But his heart was war;
His words were softer than oil,
Yet they were drawn swords (vv. 20-21).

Finally the psalm gives a blessed word of comfort and conviction, a word that is fitting for anyone of faith who may read these words during the coming days of despair. These words tell of a brighter day yet to come, a day of victory for the Jewish people, a day when "men of bloodshed and deceit will not live out half their days."

> Cast your burden upon the LORD and He will
> sustain you;
> He will never allow the righteous to be shaken.
> But You, O God, will bring them down to
> the pit of destruction;
> Men of bloodshed and deceit will not live out
> half their days
> But I will trust in You (vv. 22-23).

This fascinating psalm delivers a prophetic word picture of things to come. The Jewish heart will be longing to be set free from persecution, looking for a place of rest when, finally, the enemy is defeated and "men of bloodshed and deceit will not live out half their days," a reference to the millennial kingdom.

But before the millennium, consider the one who brings such persecution on the Jew.

Verses 12-14 speak of this evil one as an insider. The writers give the cry of a broken heart, "If it had been an enemy, I could handle that, buy you are a man my equal, my companion and friend." Later, in verse 20, the psalm speaks of the Antichrist as one who "put forth his hands against those who were at peace with him," and, most telling, "He has violated his covenant." How did he do this? It was not the sheer force of brute power but rather "his speech was smoother than butter. . . . His words were softer than oil" (v. 21). In the end his destination is "the pit of destruction" (v. 23).

From the heart of a Jew, persecuted by one of his own, betrayed by one who should protect, the psalmist records his cries of pain about the coming Antichrist.

These words could describe any traitor, like Judas, but they are specific enough in detail to describe the ultimate double crosser, the Antichrist himself. Like Judas, of whom Jesus referred in John 6:70 when He said "one of you is a devil," the Antichrist has the same satanic personality and is under the same control.

Chapter 5

Satanic by Origin

His earthly origins may trace back to Abraham, but do not be deceived, his real father is the devil himself.

Both the Old and New Testaments testify of the authority behind the Antichrist. Daniel the prophet says, "His power will be mighty, but not by his own power, and he will destroy to an extraordinary degree and prosper and perform his will; he will destroy mighty men and the holy people" (Dan. 8:24). Great power, "but not by his own power." He will destroy the "mighty men and the holy people" by the power of Satan.

In the New Testament, John was given the revelation of the beast, who was the Antichrist. About this conglomeration of Daniel's prophecy—a beast who was like a leopard, a lion, and a bear—John says that "the dragon gave him his power and his throne and great authority" (Rev. 13:2). Who is the dragon? Of course, it is the devil.

Why does the devil incarnate himself into the Antichrist rather than just appear as the Satan himself? Because the devil is the great imitator of God! The devil mimics the actions of God the Father because he wants to deceive the world. Jesus said of Himself, "Do you not believe that I am in the Father, and the Father is in Me? The words that I say to you I do not speak on My own initiative, but the Father abiding in Me does His works" (John 14:10). In his concluding remarks to His followers, Jesus stated that "all authority has been given to Me in heaven and on earth" (Matt. 28:18).

Satan decided to resemble God in every way, and displaying himself in human form as the Antichrist is his means of deception. Why does he do this? Not just because he wants to *be* God. Satan is already aware that he has lost that battle. Now his motive is to take as many down with him as possible. Rather than trying to *be* God, he wants to convince others that he *is* God, using deception, disguise, and emulation.

So the "son of perdition" comes "in accord with the activity of Satan" and, as his son, comes with "all power and signs and false wonders" (2 Thess. 2:9). Read it clearly: as Jesus is to the Father, so the Antichrist is to Satan! The Antichrist is as identical in characteristics to his father, Satan, as Jesus is to His Father, Almighty God.

Consider the comparison of the Antichrist to Satan given in the Revelation:

Satan, the dragon, is described in Revelation 12:3: "Then another sign appeared in heaven: and behold, a great red dragon having seven heads and ten horns, and on his heads were seven diadems."

The Antichrist, the beast, is described in Revelation 13:1, "And the dragon stood on the sand of the seashore. Then I saw a beast coming up out of the sea, having ten horns and seven heads, and on his horns were ten diadems, and on his heads were blasphemous names."

Notice that both the dragon (Satan) and the beast (Anitchrist) have seven heads and ten horns. Now consider the likeness of Jesus to the Father: "And He is the radiance of His glory and the exact representation of His nature, and upholds all things by the word of His power. When He had made purification of sins, He sat down at the right hand of the Majesty on high" (Heb. 1:3).

This likeness, this "incarnation" is a fulfillment of that earliest end-times prophecy that began our study, Genesis 3:15, "And I will put enmity between you and the woman, and between your seed and her seed; he shall bruise you on the head, and you shall bruise him on the heel."

The phrase "your seed and her seed" is important. Satan's seed is the Antichrist. The woman's seed is the Virgin-born Son of God, from whom the ultimate victory would come.

Humanism is a great curse and one of the biggest lies of our day. Each time I walk into a public school, and unfortunately many times in unthinking churches, I find "encouraging" signs that are humanistic to the core. Signs proclaiming "You can do whatever you set out to do," or "If you think it, you can do it." Humanism is the idea that the human mind, body, and spirit has no limits and can accomplish whatever it sets out to accomplish. "The Secret" by Rhonda Byrne, and promoted by Oprah, is a prime example of humanism in our society today.

Humanism is not our biggest problem! Our bigger problem is outside the control of the human spirit—the forces of darkness that are at work in the world today. In the days of the Antichrist, the forces of darkness will be allowed nearly full reign as "the restrainer" is removed, and will work his evil upon the world, bringing it to the brink of collapse.

Why does the devil not incarnate himself in the Antichrist now? Because God will not let him! Today good exists alongside evil. The world has seen the incarnation of God in Jesus Christ and someday will be allowed to see the incarnation of Satan in the Antichrist. The Spirit of God is the one "who now restrains" (2 Thess. 2:7), and He will do so until God the Father gives the order to get out of the way. Any casual student of prophecy can see that God is already paving the way.

Chapter 6

His Identity

The identity of the Antichrist is only understood with the careful study of four visions the Old Testament prophet Daniel received while in exile in Babylon. Daniel was given four visions, which, taken together, give a strikingly clear portrait of the identity of the Antichrist.

First, let's take a look at each vision, one of which we encountered in chapter 2. After seeing the visions, we will make application that will draw the picture of the Man of Sin.

The Colossus: Daniel 2:31-43

This vision of Nebuchadnezzar, king of Babylon, was revealed to Daniel, who had heavenly insight to interpret it to the king, Daniel's boss. Nebuchadnezzar is actually a foreshadowing or type of Antichrist. He took the place of God and forced others to bow down to his statue in worship of the king. Daniel's friends, Shadrach, Meshach, and Abenego, defied the order, just as a remnant of Jews will do in the final days. They were rewarded with the fiery furnace and then with the Son of God Himself! This is a striking picture of the future when brave Jewish believers will stand firm against the Antichrist and be rewarded with the real Christ!

Nebuchadnezzar's vision was of a giant statue (perhaps this is where he dreamed up the idea of a giant Nebuchadnezzar!). Often called "The Colossus," this statue represented four kingdoms.

The head of gold pictured Nebuchadnezzar and the Babylonian Kingdom. The shoulders and arms of silver represented the two-armed kingdom of the Medes and the Persians. The abdomen of brass represented the coming kingdom of Alexander the Great and the Greek Empire. Finally, the legs of iron and feet of clay pictured the Roman Empire. This empire ended with the ten toes, represented elsewhere as ten horns, which are ten kingdoms. An often forgotten kingdom in this vision is the most important, however!

In the days of those kings the God of heaven will set up a kingdom which will never be destroyed, and that kingdom will not be left for another people; it will crush and put an end to all these kingdoms, but it will itself endure forever. Inasmuch as you saw that a stone was cut out of the mountain without hands and that it crushed the iron, the bronze, the clay, the silver and the gold, the great God has made known to the king what will take place in the future; so the dream is true and its interpretation is trustworthy (Dan. 2:44-45).

Someday a Stone will break the coming ten toes, and that Stone will set up the word's fifth empire—the millennial kingdom. As this fifth empire becomes reality, the stone which the builders rejected will become the Chief Cornerstone, both physically and spiritually.

The vision of the Colossus is, in a sense, a short history of the world. Note the deterioration of society and of strength as time progresses. Moving from gold to silver to brass to iron to clay, society is pictured as getting weaker, not stronger. This weakness of strength is shown in governmental control as well. King Nebuchadnezzar had full control, even to the point of being worshipped. King Darius of the coming Persian Kingdom, however, did not even have the power to remove Daniel from the lion's den. The Greek Empire was held together only by sheer military might, and was so frail that when its young leader was poisoned the empire immediately began to deteriorate. Finally Rome came and became the first empire to be run by committee!

Note also that the second kingdom had two arms, the Medes and the Persians. The final kingdom of Rome, then, was one unit at first, in the lower torso of the figure, but then was divided into two legs, representing the two branches (East and West) of the Roman Empire, and then, ultimately, into ten kingdoms.

The Four Beasts: Daniel 7

Mentioned previously, this vision gives further insight into the vision of the Colossus. As previously considered, this vision also shows four worldwide empires, beginning with Babylon. Even today, if you perform an Internet search of "Babylon Lion" you will get millions of pages of text and pictures connecting the lion with the empire of Babylon in

Nebuchadnezzar's day. The lion was the indisputable symbol of the empire.

The next beast in the vision was a lopsided bear, representing the Medo-Persian Empire. This bear, raised on one side, shows the strength of the Persians over the Medes yet the union of the two. The three ribs likely represent Lydia, Babylon, and Egypt, the three nations that once formed an alliance against Persia and lost.

The leopard with four wings represents the Greek Kingdom. A leopard is one of the swiftest animals of creation on its own, but add four wings and it becomes historically swift, much like the empire of Alexander the Great. In a matter of months, Alexander overtook the Persian Empire. Having four heads, the beast represents the four kingdoms which would come out of the Greek Kingdom upon Alexander's early death.

Rome was pictured by a beast unlike any other, only to be described as "dreadful and terrifying." In this vision we see ten horns, corresponding to the ten toes of the Colossus. Here we learn that these represent ten kingdoms.

The Ram and the Goat: Daniel 8

In this third insightful vision, Daniel sees a ram of two horns, representing the kingdom of the Medes and Persians. This ram was powerful, expanding his territory in all directions. But then came swiftly a male goat with a large horn to attack the ram. While the ram should have prevailed, the goat won the battle, and the ram quickly succumbed. Then an interesting turn of events occurred. As quickly as the goat prevailed, the large horn was broken and replaced with four horns. This is a clear picture of Alexander the Great and his kingdom. "As soon as he was mighty" (Dan. 8:8), Alexander died at the age of thirty-three. Not having prepared a plan of succession, his kingdom was broken into four divisions, the kingdoms of Thrace, Macedonia, Syria, and Egypt.

The identity of these horns is important to the location of the origin of the future Antichrist.

The vision showed that out of these four horns, one began "rather small" but grew to be "exceedingly great" toward the "Beautiful Land" (v. 9). This rather small horn is the Antichrist, as we will explain later.

A large number of Bible students claim that the prophecy of the small horn was fulfilled in Antiochus Ephiphanes, king of Syria. Indeed Antiochus Epiphanies was a foreshadow of the Anitchrist, and the fact that he was king of Syria fits the vision, Syria being one of the four kingdoms represented by the four horns. This evil king became strong and brought his terror into the "Beautiful Land" of Jerusalem, even sacrificing a pig on the altar, desecrating it.

While Antiochus may be the preliminary shadow of fulfillment, he cannot be the ultimate fulfillment because he does not fulfill the prophecy completely. Consider that the small horn goes against "the Prince of princes" (v. 25) who is Jesus Christ, something Antiochus never did. Further, the small horn was

81

prophesied to be "broken without human agency," but Antiochus was never broken, rather dying a natural death. While the desecration of the pig may have been a foreshadowing of the abomination of desecration, Jesus referred to that event as a future event, further disqualifying Antiochus as the ultimate fulfillment of Daniel 8.

By now you may be asking how this little horn of four horns in Daniel 8 could be the same as the little horn of ten horns given in Daniel 7. Rest assured that the ten horns are inclusive of the four.

The Kings of the North and South: Daniel 11

The final vision, received fifteen years after the vision of Daniel 8, solves the mystery of the identity of the kingdom represented by the forth horn from which the Antichrist arose.

Daniel 11 is one of the most difficult passages of prophecy in the entire Bible. Theologians debate whether all of it or none of it has been fulfilled.

Most fall somewhere in the middle, with verses 1-20 or 1-35 describing past events and 21 (or 36) and beyond describing future events. Undisputed among dispensationalists is the conviction that verses 36-45 describe the Antichrist.

> Then the king will do as he pleases, and he will exalt and magnify himself above every god and will speak monstrous things against the God of gods; and he will prosper until the indignation is finished, for that which is decreed will be done. He will show no regard for the gods of his fathers or for the desire of women, nor will he show regard for any other god; for he will magnify himself above them all. But instead he will honor a god of fortresses, a god whom his fathers did not know; he will honor him with gold, silver, costly stones and treasures. He will take action against the strongest of fortresses with the help of a foreign god; he will give great

honor to those who acknowledge him and will cause them to rule over the many, and will parcel out land for a price. At the end time the king of the South will collide with him, and the king of the North will storm against him with chariots, with horsemen and with many ships; and he will enter countries, overflow them and pass through. He will also enter the Beautiful Land, and many countries will fall; but these will be rescued out of his hand: Edom, Moab and the foremost of the sons of Ammon. Then he will stretch out his hand against other countries, and the land of Egypt will not escape. But he will gain control over the hidden treasures of gold and silver and over all the precious things of Egypt; and Libyans and Ethiopians will follow at his heels. But rumors from the East and from the North will disturb him, and he will go forth with great wrath to destroy and annihilate many. He will pitch the tents of his royal pavilion between the seas and the beautiful Holy Mountain; yet he will come to his end, and no one will help him (Dan. 11:36-45).

This graphic picture of the Antichrist will be considered in greater detail later, but it gives us one important clue about the Antichrist—*where he comes from!*

We already know his race. Now we know he is "the king of the North." What does this mean?

These visions narrow the identity of the Antichrist to one who is of Jewish ancestry and an Assyrian ruler of the Gentile world!

The vision of the ram and the goat is a vision of the Greek Kingdom; this vision identifies the Antichrist as having a Greek heritage. The visions of the kings of the North and South narrow that to the Syrian region of the Greek Empire because the Syrian king is the indisputable "king of the North" in the fourfold division of Alexander's empire. Thus we know that the Antichrist will be a Jewish male coming from the new Roman Empire, specifically from the region of the Seleucid Kingdom in the area of Syria and the ancient Assyrian Empire.

How does a Jewish male become the ruler of Syria (or a nation in the region of Syria), then revive much of Alexander's kingdom and eventually become the last Caesar of the Roman Empire? Stay tuned!

Chapter 7

His Kingdom

A Jewish male from the region of Syria ascends to prominence among the descendents of the Greek and Roman Empires. By his smooth words and suave style, he gains an increasing level of power, both the authority of office and the power of persuasion. In the end he becomes the most powerful world leader history has ever seen.

How could it happen?

A Time of Gaining

Every trailblazer needs time to mature. Often the young make hasty decisions based on limited knowledge and experience. Their worldview changes through experience—their opinion of people, their black-and-white viewpoints, their firm convictions that later may be found to be based on incomplete information. These things change, and often should, over time.

Any mature believer understands this process. We all look back with amazement on some of the follies of our youth! Each year we live, we seem to discover more of our ignorance!

The world has come to expect that a time of maturity is needed and, odd as it may seem, will even require that of the Antichrist. Perhaps coming on the scene at a young age, this Man of Sin will have to earn his followers through proven strategies and real accomplishments. Even flowery speeches will only get you a limited distance with a scrutinizing public.

The Antichrist will have an unspecified period of time immediately after the rapture in which he is gaining in popularity and power. Do not be deceived by the oft taught but overly simplified teaching that the tribulation begins immediately after the rapture, and that seven years to the day will mark the second coming of Christ! I maintain that there is some period of time between the rapture and the official beginning of the tribulation.

How long? It is hard to say! Much depends on how much groundwork is set in place for the tribulation before the rapture.

For example, if you study teachers of biblical prophecy writing before 1920, you will find that almost entirely this group of theologians taught that after the rapture Jews would return to Israel and that nation would be established as a Jewish state. However, as I write these words, Israel is in the midst of celebrating its sixtieth anniversary as a Jewish state. These teachers of old were mistaken because they failed to consider that much but not all the groundwork for the tribulation can be concluded before the rapture begins.

If the rapture were to take place today (Come quickly, Lord Jesus!), it would probably be years before the official timekeeper of the tribulation begins his work. This time period before the start of the tribulation would likely include the war of Ezekiel 38–39 followed by the rebuilding of the Jewish temple, which must be completed before the midpoint of the tribulation, for that is where the Antichrist will perform the "abomination of desolation" spoken of by Daniel and Jesus.

This indefinite period of time is also the period of the removal of the restraint that currently holds evil in check: "For the mystery of lawlessness is already at work; only he who now restrains will do so until he is taken out of the way. Then that lawless one will be revealed whom the Lord will slay with the breath of His mouth and bring to an end by the appearance of His coming" (2 Thess. 2:7-8).

There have been at least four interpretations for the identity of "he who now restrains."

1. Some believe it is Satan himself. This hardly makes sense when one considers that Satan would be restraining himself.

2. Other's favor human government. Usually this bunch reads the Scripture allegorically and sees the day coming when government will fail and no longer be able to provide the restraint for evil that it now does. The problem is twofold. First, government has through the ages been the cause of evil, not the cure. The most atrocious acts of mankind through the centuries of history have been performed by governors and governments. Second, human government has no power over spiritual forces. To think that a man-made institution could have influence on the spiritual forces of darkness is a dangerous arrogance.

3. Others believe the New Testament church is "he who now restrains." These would remind us that the church will be removed with the rapture and that only the church has been promised that "the gates of hell shall not prevail against it." With the removal of this spiritually powerful organization, Satan will have the opportunity to send his Antichrist. While this view has advantages, I side with those who hold to the final interpretation.

4. The Holy Spirit is the true restrainer. Only God in the Holy Spirit has the power to overcome the forces of evil found in Satan. Only God can keep Satan on a leash, and Scripture teaches that He does so. When God chooses, and at God's time, He will remove His Spirit from His restraining role, and "all hell will break loose."

It is only the restraining role of the Spirit that ceases. The Spirit of God will still be on the Earth. The Spirit will still convict some of sin, judgment, and righteousness. The Spirit will still empower some to come to Christ, and those who do will still be indwelt by the Spirit. The Spirit will perform the actions He has performed since the days of Pentecost. There is one role, however, which the Spirit will relinquish: the role of restrainer. For all of history since the garden of Eden, the Spirit of God has been holding Satan back from setting forth his satanic plan. In that day the restrainer will be removed.

This period of gaining is also a time of the rise of the old Roman Empire (assuming it does not happen in the intervening days between now and the rapture). Today the Roman Empire has not risen to the point of having at least ten discernable kings or kingdoms.

How long would this rising again take? This is anyone's guess but likely not long.

By one count twenty-eight new nations have come into being since 1990.[5] With the quick change of the map and the geopolitical structure the world has experienced since the fall of the USSR, it is not hard to imagine a quickly emerging coalition of nations and peoples of the old Roman Empire.

This period of gaining is also a time in which a Jewish, Assyrian King secures a leading role. After the rise of the ten nations of the Roman Empire, the eleventh king begins to grow from small beginnings. This eleventh king will be the Jewish king of an Assyrian nation.

Anyone who knows current events is now asking, "How does a Jew become a king anywhere near the Assyrian region?" Today's Syria, the remnants of the old Assyrian Empire, are staunch enemies of all things Jewish. In fact, Assyrians have always been enemies of the Jews.

I believe that the Ezekiel 38–39 war plays a key role in the rise of the Antichrist. It is clear in this passage that Iran and the Muslim coalition suffer a humiliating defeat. I believe God will use this war to bring the ultimate downfall of the Islamic religion and the false god Allah. With the fall of Islam, Syrian-Jewish relations have a much more likely chance of tranquility over animosity. I certainly stand in the minority today, as most teachers of prophecy believe in an Islamic antichrist.

I foresee the fall of Islam prior to the rise of the Antichrist for these reasons:

- The Ezekiel 38–39 war brings great military defeat to Islamic nations.

- The Antichrist will enter into covenant with Israel. It is almost inconceivable to imagine Israel entering into covenant with the Muslim "Mahdi."

- Scripture describes end-times Babylon as a place of every kind of sensuality (see Rev. 18:3). Sensuality and Islam do not go together. Is this a clue of the fall of Islam?

• Islam is unconditionally monotheistic. How does this line up with the Antichrist's forcing the manufacture of idols for worship?

Some of this will be discussed in future pages in more detail, but for these reasons I take a minority opinion that the Antichrist is not Muslim.

Even without this scenario, you need to understand what it takes to be Jewish.

Rabbis teach that "Jewishness" passes from *mother* to child, not from *father* to child. A child of a Jewish father and Gentile mother is a Gentile. A child of a Gentile father and Jewish mother is Jewish. This Jewish mother does not have to be a practicing Jew, but her Jewishness passes from one generation to the next.

Consider this enlightening question sent to an Internet Q&A forum on Jewish identity. The question related to proving one's Jewish identity—

Jewish identity is passed on via the mother. If the mother is Jewish, the child is 100% Jewish. This is true regardless of who the father is, and whether he is Jewish or not, and regardless of whether the Jewish mother practiced another religion. That is the unwavering rule. At the same time, if someone's father is Jewish (but not the mother), then the child is 100% NOT Jewish.

Jewish identity passed on through the mother has been universally accepted by Jews for 3,000 years. . . . According to Jewish law, this will remain the person's status forever. There is no way one can lose his status as a Jew even if he thinks he has gone so far as to convert to another religion!

Therefore, if your mother's mother's mother was Jewish, then you would also be considered Jewish. However, because of the complexity of your situation, you will need to bring proof that your mother's mother's mother (or her daughter, granddaughter etc.) was Jewish. Proof may include birth certificates, gravestones, etc. Assuming this is too far back for you to go, then your status remains as a non-Jew.

With blessings from Jerusalem,

Rabbi Shraga Simmons[6]

With this insight we see that this "king of Syria" may not be a practicing Jew and perhaps may not even realize he is a Jew until some stealth genetic research discovers a distant Jewish great-grandmother! Now, with Islam dead or dying and Israel on the rise, this king announces his Jewishness!

Daniel gives us further insight into how a Jew can become king of this Assyrian nation: "In his place a despicable person will arise, on whom the honor of kingship has not been conferred, but he will come in a time of tranquility and seize the kingdom by intrigue" (Dan. 11:21).

Don't miss it: he will "seize the kingdom by intrigue." That is, he is not a king until he uses his powers of flattery, his "smooth as butter" speech, his influence, background, and persuasion. These become his ladder to the pinnacle of success and power.

Rising to prominence, eventually three of the ten countries come under control of this "little horn." Never satisfied, he continues to work his words and word his works in such a way that his power increases, and the period of gaining gives way to the next period.

A Time of Feigning

After the time of maturity and gaining of strength, popularity, and power, the true identity of the Antichrist becomes known to those with discernment when the Assyrian establishes peace with Israel, signing the "covenant with the many" described by Daniel. Here the Antichrist begins to feign his role as the Messiah, the promised one. The covenant will be celebrated, probably worldwide, bringing the Antichrist into the international spotlight. While most of the world will celebrate this event, they will not recognize it as prophetic.

When the covenant is signed, the countdown clock begins.

Daniel speaks of a seventieth week for Israel: "And he will make a firm covenant with the many for one week, but in the middle of the week he will put a stop to sacrifice and grain offering; and on the wing of abominations will come one who makes desolate, even until a complete destruction, one that is decreed, is poured out on the one who makes desolate" (Dan. 9:27). The first sixty-nine of the seventy promised weeks for Israel have already been accomplished, but then the clock stopped, and we have been living in a parenthetical period between the sixty-ninth and seventieth weeks.

John begins his revelation of the seventieth week in Revelation 6. In this chapter the book or scroll begins to be opened, one seal at a time. When the first of seven seals is broken, the Antichrist comes in on a white horse, looking as if he were the Messiah coming to rescue the Earth. At this point many Jews love him, and soon he will enter into Jerusalem, and many more Jews will accept him as their long-awaited promised one.

Biblical prophecy is exact in its predictions, but it is not easy to be exact in understanding biblical prophecy! Rarely does one Bible prophecy contain the entire picture. Rather, if a scene has four parts, two may be in one Scripture while the other two are independent in separate Scriptures. It is left to the student of the Bible, rightly dividing the Word of truth under the leadership and guidance of the Spirit, to place these pieces of the puzzle together to complete the picture.

I believe that the pieces of the puzzle show that the Antichrist will enter Jerusalem as its king exactly 220 days after the signing of the covenant of peace. Follow the trail with me to come to this day of his arrival as king exactly seven months and ten days (using a biblical thirty-day calendar) after the signing of the peace treaty.

The Antichrist, before he begins a pogrom of Jewish destruction, will be accepted by many Jews as their Messiah. For centuries they have been longing for the one who would set them free, but when "he came unto his own, . . . his own received him not" (John 1:11, KJV).

I believe every Christian would benefit greatly from a trip to the Holy Land. Not long ago I was in Jerusalem teaching from Isaiah 53. After the teaching, I asked our Jewish guide, a beloved friend and true student of the Old Testament, what the Jewish people thought of passages like Isaiah 53 that seem to point so clearly toward Jesus. His words to me were memorable. "I believe Jesus *probably* is the Messiah. He fulfills all the prophecies of the Old Testament." But then he went on to say, "There is no way we can *know for sure* that He is the Messiah until He comes into Jerusalem and establishes His kingdom."

That is what the Jewish people are waiting for. That is why they rejected Him the first time. And, sadly, that is why many will receive the Antichrist as the Christ.

To be accepted as Messiah, the Antichrist will enter Jerusalem in an imitation of Zechariah 9:9-10:

Rejoice greatly, O daughter of Zion!
Shout in triumph, O daughter of Jerusalem!
Behold, your king is coming to you;
He is just and endowed with salvation,
Humble, and mounted on a donkey,
Even on a colt, the foal of a donkey.
I will cut off the chariot from Ephraim
And the horse from Jerusalem;
And the bow of war will be cut off
And He will speak peace to the nations;
And His dominion will be from sea to sea,
And from the River to the ends of the earth.

The Antichrist will have already established peace between Israel and the rest of the world, which will make him a hero; but it will not make him a King. He will not become king of Israel and take the throne of David until later, but this must happen by the midpoint of the tribulation.

Daniel 8:14 has an interesting word that has perplexed many, "He said to me, 'For 2,300 evenings and mornings; then the holy place will be properly restored.'" To understand how this reveals that the Antichrist will become king seven months and ten days after the signing of the peace covenant, we need to study the context of Daniel 8:14. Follow me as we look at Daniel 8:9-14 verse by verse.

Out of one of them came forth a rather small horn which grew exceedingly great toward the south, toward the east, and toward the Beautiful Land (v. 9).

The "rather small horn" is an unmistakable reference to the Antichrist. The "Beautiful Land" is the promised land of Israel.

It grew up to the host of heaven and caused some of the host and some of the stars to fall to the earth, and it trampled them down (v. 10).

This small horn, the Antichrist, "grew up to the host of heaven." Who is "the host of heaven"? Some of "the host" will fall to Earth and be trampled down by the Antichrist. The host is never a reference to God although often God is referred to as the "Lord of the host" or, as we will soon see, the "Commander of the host." Whoever the host is, it is not God; but God is the host's Lord or Commander. This means that the host must be Israel itself, the chosen people of God. So the picture in verse 8 is that the Antichrist began as a small horn but grew up even to Israel. Eventually he causes some of Israel to fall, and then he tramples them.

It even magnified itself to be equal with the Commander of the host; and it removed the regular sacrifice from Him, and the place of His sanctuary was thrown down (v. 11).

The Commander of the host is Jesus Christ Himself, the true Messiah. The Antichrist will magnify himself (with Satan's power and authority) and will remove the regular sacrifice from Jesus and direct it toward himself. Sometime before the midpoint of the tribulation, the temple will be rebuilt and sacrifice reinstituted. These sacrifices are ill intentioned because they fail to recognize the sacrifice of Jesus, the Lamb of God who takes away the sins of the world. However, the Jewish people will offer them in wholehearted devotion to God. When the Antichrist comes in as Messiah, however, he will redirect those "regular sacrifices" toward himself. This will happen initially in spirit but eventually in reality when the Antichrist takes his place in the holy of holies and sits as King David over Israel. After this time "the place of His sanctuary was thrown down." This will happen in the destruction that comes to Jerusalem and will make way for the millennial temple.

> And on account of transgression the host will be given over to the horn along with the regular sacrifice; and it will fling truth to the ground and perform its will and prosper (v. 12).

This is a sad word of the punishment for rejection that will come to "the host." Vast numbers of the Jewish people will "be given over to the horn," and "the horn" will "fling truth to the ground and perform its will and prosper."

> Then I heard a holy one speaking, and another holy one said to that particular one who was speaking, "How long will the vision about the regular sacrifice apply, while the transgression causes horror, so as to allow both

the holy place and the host to be trampled?"
(v. 13).

This is an important question for the interpretation of the next verse. Simply put, the question is, "How long will this last?" Specifically, from the time the regular sacrifices are redirected toward the Antichrist until the true Christ takes over. "How long?" Daniel 8:14 gives the answer.

He said to me, "For 2,300 evenings and mornings; then the holy place will be properly restored" (v. 14).

Now, to understand this, we need to do some math!

The seven-year covenant is 2,520 days. This is the number of days (seven years with 360 days of the biblical/Hebrew calendar) from the signing of the covenant until the second coming.

Daniel says that in twenty-three hundred days "the holy place will be properly restored." The only teaching about the holy place being restored is at the millennium, so this must be in connection with the second coming.

Now do the math: $2,520 - 2,300 = 220$. This is the number of days between the signing of the covenant and the time the regular sacrifice is given over to the Antichrist.

My Jewish friend expects a Messiah to enter Jerusalem and establish his kingdom. Unfortunately, the next one to do so, establishing a kingdom of peace, will enter into Jerusalem and be accepted as Israel's Messiah 220 days after he initiates a peace treaty with Israel. While Jesus was rejected and crucified after His entry to Jerusalem, this one will be accepted. While he will come as a man of peace, and in a time when the world rejoices of "peace and safety" (1 Thessalonians 5:3), many Jews will ultimately be taken captive by the deceptive philosophies and outright lies of this Man of Sin. Sadly, many of these Jews will not live to see the day when the real Messiah, Jesus Christ, returns and enters Jerusalem to establish His kingdom.

Today is the day to accept Jesus as the Messiah. Those who wait for His arrival in Jerusalem will wait too long. Between now and then a despicable monster will come dressed as a knight in shining armor and will deceive many.

This brings us to the final period of the Antichrist.

A Time of Reigning

After he has taken his throne, the knight in shining armor turns monstrous.

The Antichrist becomes known to the discerning when he signs the peace covenant with Israel. He becomes accepted as the Jewish Messiah 220 days later. But 1,260 days into the covenant is another important date; on this day the Antichrist cuts off sacrifices altogether and in the temple sets himself up as God. This is the "Abomination of Desolation." On this day the Antichrist changes from friend to foe, from "messiah" to maniac. Only three and a half years after an unprecedented peace begins, an unprecedented war against the Jews begins by the peacemaker himself.

Jesus gives stern warning to the Jews on what to do in that day: GET OUT.

Then those who are in Judea must flee to the mountains. Whoever is on the housetop must not go down to get the things out that are in his house. Whoever is in the field must not turn back to get his cloak. But woe to those who are pregnant and to those who are nursing babies in those days! But pray that your flight will not be in the winter, or on a Sabbath. For then there will be a great tribulation, such as has not occurred since the beginning of the world until now, nor ever will (Matt. 24:16-21).

How drastic is the need to flee? How dangerous is this to the Jew? How bad does it get?

Unless those days had been cut short, no life would have been saved; but for the sake of the elect those days will be cut short (Matt. 24:22).

I worry about men like Mahmoud Ahmadenijad—not because I fear he is the Antichrist, for he certainly is not—but because he holds an Antichrist spirit of destruction of the Jews and the Jewish nation of Israel. Jews bear the name of Jehovah in their very being, and so their existence is a threat to all who carry the spirit of the Antichrist. Jews bear the emblem of the living God; they are the chosen of God Almighty, and the apple of His eye. For this reason all those who are on the side of Satan hate Jews, and all who hate Jews are on the side of Satan.

So the Jews on that day will flee to the mountains, crying:

> O God, do not remain quiet;
> Do not be silent and, O God, do not be still.
> For behold, Your enemies make an uproar,
> And those who hate You have exalted
>   themselves.
> They make shrewd plans against Your people,
> And conspire together against Your treasured
>   ones.
> They have said, "Come, and let us wipe them
>   out as a nation,
> That the name of Israel be remembered no
>   more" (Ps. 83:1-4).

Interestingly, during this time a remnant of the people of God will become His again.

Chapter 8

A Remnant Saved

During their run from the Antichrist, God is going to do a great work among the Jewish people, and many will be saved.

Paul's Prayer

The apostle Paul was as Jewish as they come and had a firm understanding of Jewish theology and the mind of God as it relates to Israel. Paul expressed the mind of God when he said, "My heart's desire and my prayer for them is for their salvation" (Rom. 10:1). This prayer is expressed in the center of Paul's theological statement on the condition of the Jews. Romans 9–11 has been called "God's Position Paper on Israel." Such a designation accurately describes these three chapters.

These chapters begin with a clear reminder that God is sovereign and can do whatever He wants to do! In the plan of God, He chose a group of people—the children of Abraham—as His chosen. But Paul is specific that not *all* of Abraham's children are chosen but those of Isaac alone (Rom. 9:6-7). Then Paul further reminds us that not *all* of Isaac's children are chosen but those of Jacob alone (Rom. 9:10-13). Paul goes through this narrowing to show us that the rejection of Christ by the Jews does not necessitate the rejection of the Jews by God! God can do as He pleases, and it pleases God to save a remnant from Israel, out of the coming tribulation, who will, in totality, be saved. Paul is specific when he proclaims that "it does not depend on the man who wills or the man who runs, but on God who has mercy" (Rom. 9:16).

God has tucked away enough of a remnant of the Jews through history that, despite the endless persecutions and pogroms against them, some have always remained. In spite of impossible odds, a cohesive group has kept their identity (something no other family of peoples has done when removed from their homeland). The current remnant of Jews is in view of the coming remnant that will be saved through the tribulation. When the tribulation is over, after the wholesale slaughter of millions of Jews, there will be a saved remnant, and "all Israel will be saved" (Rom. 11:26).

Praying the Psalms

During this time of fleeing Jerusalem and the Antichrist, I believe the Jews will, in large numbers, turn to Jesus Christ as the Messiah. As they are fleeing, they will be praying the Psalms of Ascent (Psalms 121–134). These fifteen psalms played an important role in Jewish life in temple days, likely used as prayers and songs of Jews as they approached the city of Jerusalem and the temple of God.

But in coming days, these psalms will take on special significance. If they are read in light of the persecution of the Antichrist and the fleeing of Jerusalem, they bring about an eerie realization of the coming persecution. When these psalms are read from the point of view of a Jew who loves Jerusalem but is fleeing for his life and that of his family, they are powerful prayers for deliverance and longing for peace. As the faithful Jew flees, he has renounced all pride, wisdom, allegiance to worldly powers, and dependence on worldly wealth. Instead he is completely trusting on the saving power of Almighty God, and these psalms become his prayer book and worship guide as he flees for his life and runs to the Lord.

Following directly through the Psalms of Ascent, used in ancient times as prayers of progression toward the temple, consider them now as prayers of agony and longing for the hand of God to redeem them from the hand of the Antichrist.

As the remnant Jew flees westward into the Judean mountains, his prayer is, "I will lift up my eyes to the mountains; from where shall my help come?" (Ps. 121:1). While running from Jerusalem, his prayer is, "[I] Pray for the peace of Jerusalem. . . . May peace be within your walls, and prosperity within your palaces. For the sake of my brothers and my friends, I will now say, 'May peace be within you'" (Ps. 122:6-8).

Continuing to run, he declares, along with his fellow Jews, that his sight will not depart from the God of Israel. "Behold, as the eyes of servants look to the hand of their master, as the eyes of a maid to the hand of her mistress, so our eyes look to the LORD our God, until He is gracious to us. Be gracious to us, LORD, . . . for we are greatly filled with contempt" (Ps. 123:2-3).

The escapee now gives praise for the way in which the Lord miraculously spared them from the wrath of Antichrist. "'Had it not been the LORD who was on our side,' let Israel now say, . . . 'When men rose up against us, then they would have swallowed us alive.' . . . Blessed be the LORD, who has not give us to be torn by their teeth. Our soul has escaped as a bird out of the snare of the trapper" (Ps. 124:1-3, 6-7).

Even though barely escaping with his life, the Jew never falters in his faith in the promises of God. He rejoices that, "the scepter of wickedness shall not rest upon the land of the righteous, so that the righteous will not put forth their hands to do wrong" (Ps. 125:3.) In this prayer he is beginning to look toward the future, when God shall save His people! Considering this future, he is reminded that "those who sow in tears shall reap with joyful shouting. He who goes to and fro weeping, carrying his bag of seed, shall indeed come again with a shout of joy, bringing his sheaves with him" (Ps. 126:5-6).

Moving forward, the fleeing Jew rejoices again in the strength of the Lord. Though the government of

Israel has not been able to bring protection, the God of Israel will accomplish the Peace of Jerusalem! "Unless the LORD builds the house, they labor in vain who build it; unless the LORD guards the city, the watchman keeps awake in vain" (Ps. 127:1). Even though he is in the midst of the worst persecution, his hope is still in the Lord as he prays, "The LORD bless you from Zion, and may you see the prosperity of Jerusalem. . . . Indeed, may you see your children's children. Peace be upon Israel!" (Ps. 128:5-6).

Remembering the horrific history of Israel's persecution, the Jew prays, "'Many times they have persecuted me from my youth up,' let Israel now say, 'Yet they have not prevailed against me." . . . May all who hate Zion be put to shame and turned backward; let them be like grass upon the housetops, which withers before it grows up" (Ps. 129:1-2, 5-6). And in the depths of persecution, he prays, "Out of the depths I have cried to You, O LORD. Lord, hear my voice! Let Your ears be attentive to the voice of my supplications" (Ps. 130:1-2). Never giving up, he continues, "O Israel, hope in the LORD from this time forth and forever" (Ps. 131:3), and, "Remember, O LORD, on David's behalf, all his affliction" (Ps. 132:1).

As the Lord begins to do a miraculous spiritual work among His people, the Jew, now having had a spiritual experience under the hand of the Messiah, rejoices, saying, "Behold, how good and how pleasant it is for brothers to dwell together in unity!" (Ps. 133:1). And seeing the hand of the Lord redeeming His people, knowing that the salvation of the Lord is near, the remnant of Jews now proclaims victory, saying, "Lift up your hands to the sanctuary and bless the LORD. May the LORD bless you from Zion, He who made heaven and earth" (Ps. 134:2-3).

John's Vision

When the apostle John, who was imprisoned in the Alcatraz of his day on the island of Patmos, received a vision of the end, one of the most memorable aspects of this vision was the witness of 144,000 sealed members of the army of God and "two olive trees" or "two lampstands" often referred to as the two witnesses. The 144,000 are clearly identified as Jews, and they are clearly and completely protected from the wrongdoing of the Antichrist. God handpicks twelve thousand from each tribe of Israel (He has not "lost" the ten tribes!) and seals them for service. He also sends His two witnesses (many say they are Elijah and Moses, as seen on the Mount of Transfiguration) for three and a half years of ministry.

These witnesses and this mighty army are endowed with God's power to proclaim God's truth in unmistakable ways. As a result of their God-ordained ministry, many Jews and Gentiles will be saved. John sees "a great multitude which no one could count" (Rev. 7:9) who have received Christ as Savior and subsequently lost their lives in the days of tribulation.

God uses the work of these 144,000 and the two witnesses to bring about His remnant so that a multitude is saved and a great, worldwide revival takes place even in the midst of the death and destruction of the reign of the Man of Sin.

Chapter 9

Babylon, the Rebellious City

Babylon, the city that has been largely in ruins for centuries, is the most recognizable ancient city in the world. Even though long dead and gone, it lives on. It is the epitome of cosmopolitan living and humanistic thought. If Hollywood means ego and New York is greed, then Babylon is arrogance with a capital A!

The arrogance is seen in Babylon's founder, Nimrod.

The name *Nimrod* has often been misunderstood by modern readers of the Bible. Nimrod is said to have been one who was a "mighty hunter" or a "mighty warrior" (Gen. 10:8-11). In this light the name *Nimrod* has been used by schools as a mascot (a Peabody Award went to the makers of *Nimrod Nation* for the documentary on the Waterstreet High School Nimrods). The name is used by the University of Tulsa for its *International Journal of Prose and Poetry*. Cape Cod is home to the Nimrod Restaurant, a place of "innovative and traditional cuisine in a relaxed and elegant milieu."[7] An area outside of Little Rock, Arkansas, is named Nimrod. NIMROD is an acronym for "Non-Ideal Magnetohydrodynamics with Rotation Open Discussion." In case that doesn't mean anything to you, here is the NIMROD project made simple —

NIMROD project is to develop a modern computer code suitable for the study of long-wavelength, low-frequency, nonlinear phenomena in realistic toroidal geom-etry, including Tokamaks, Spheromaks, Reversed Field Pinches, and Field-Reversed

Configurations, making use of a multi-disciplinary, multi-institutional team, and making the final code available to the whole fusion community.[8]

Well, I admit, it means nothing to me either!

Mascots, journals, restaurants, communities, scientific and computer projects, and more! In fact, there are even numerous churches named Nimrod!

But is the name something to be proud of? While most men would be honored to be called "mighty hunter" or "mighty warrior," the name itself is not flattering. *Nimrod* means "rebel" or "rebellion."

Genesis 10:8-9 reads: "Now Cush became the father of Nimrod; he became a mighty one on the earth. He was a mighty hunter before the LORD; therefore it is said, 'Like Nimrod a mighty hunter before the LORD.'" But this great-grandson of Noah was not a mighty hunter *for* the Lord, or a mighty soldier in the Lord's army. Literally, the Hebrew says that Nimrod ("Rebel") was a mighty hunter "before the

Lord's face," meaning that this rebel was so arrogant he was willing to put his fist in the face of God.

Did Nimrod "the rebel" rebel against God? Consider the instruction God gave to Noah: "As for you, be fruitful and multiply; populate the earth abundantly and multiply in it" (Gen. 9:7).

Once again this Scripture is clearer in Hebrew where "be fruitful" and "populate" have a clear implication to "spread out" and "swarm" the earth. Rather than spread out, Nimrod gathered in and built himself a city and a kingdom; the land of Babylon was born.

Having rebelled against the command of the Lord, Nimrod's city of Babylon went further to show arrogance in building a tower to "make for ourselves a name" so that they would not be "scattered abroad over the face of the whole earth" (Gen. 11:4). In other words, the tower itself was a fist in the face of God, saying, "You told us to scatter, but we refuse. This tower will forever unify us around our mighty strength, and we shall live without You." It is no wonder the tower of Babel is remembered to this day as a place of scattering.

Through the years, built by an arrogant founder and filled with an arrogant, godless population, Babylon became the world's most fantastic city. Babylon would later overthrow the nation of Judah, at its zenith under Nebuchadnezzar, who had made Babylon a showpiece for the world and built one of the ancient wonders of the world within its gates, the hanging gardens of Babylon.

Alexander the Great died in the city of Babylon, and after that the city began to experience a slow decline. But do not be fooled, the city lives on, and the structures shall once again stand!

The City in Prophecy

There are three key areas of prophecy concerning the city of Babylon.

First, Scripture was clear that Babylon would become a city of punishment for the Jews.

At that time Berodach-baladan a son of
Baladan, king of Babylon, sent letters and
a present to Hezekiah, for he heard that
Hezekiah had been sick. Hezekiah listened
to them, and showed them all his trea-
sure house, the silver and the gold and the
spices and the precious oil and the house of
his armor and all that was found in his treasuries. There was nothing in his house nor in
all his dominion that Hezekiah did not show
them. Then Isaiah the prophet came to King
Hezekiah and said to him, "What did these
men say, and from where have they come to
you?" And Hezekiah said, "They have come
from a far country, from Babylon." He said,
"What have they seen in your house?" So
Hezekiah answered, "They have seen all that
is in my house; there is nothing among my
treasuries that I have not shown them." Then
Isaiah said to Hezekiah, "Hear the word of
the LORD. 'Behold, the days are coming when

all that is in your house, and all that your
fathers have laid up in store to this day will
be carried to Babylon; nothing shall be left,'
says the LORD. 'Some of your sons who shall
issue from you, whom you will beget, will be
taken away; and they will become officials in
the palace of the king of Babylon'" (2 Kings
20:12-18).

This prophecy was fulfilled in the days of Daniel,
when Daniel and his generation were carried off to
Babylon and experienced a seventy-year punishment (a prophetic time of fulfilling the Sabbath rest
commanded by the Lord but ignored by His people).
During this time Judah mourned for her homeland
and the city of Jerusalem.

By the rivers of Babylon,
There we sat down and wept,
When we remembered Zion.
Upon the willows in the midst of it

We hung our harps.

For there our captors demanded of us songs,

And our tormentors mirth, saying,

"Sing us one of the songs of Zion."

How can we sing the LORD's song

In a foreign land? (Ps. 137:1-4).

The next prophecy is of a Babylon of the last days, which is a city of power, prestige, and sensuality. John saw the city of Babylon, alive and well, in the revelation of last things. Here is his description: "The woman was clothed in purple and scarlet, and adorned with gold and precious stones and pearls, having in her hand a gold cup full of abominations and of the unclean things of her immorality" (Rev. 17:4).

John continues to tell us that this "woman" was Babylon. Notice her purple, scarlet, gold, precious stones, pearls, and immorality. Continue to notice the power, prestige, and sensuality as John describes her fall:

And the merchants of the earth weep and mourn over her, because no one buys their cargoes any more— cargoes of gold and silver and precious stones and pearls and fine linen and purple and silk and scarlet, and every kind of citron wood and every article of ivory and every article made from very costly wood and bronze and iron and marble, and cinnamon and spice and incense and perfume and frankincense and wine and olive oil and fine flour and wheat and cattle and sheep, and cargoes of horses and chariots and slaves and human lives. The fruit you long for has gone from you, and all things that were luxurious and splendid have passed away from you and men will no longer find them. The merchants of these things, who became rich from her, will stand at a distance because of the fear of her torment, weeping and mourning (Rev. 18:11-15).

From this description of prosperity, which describes the end-times Babylon, we clearly should expect Babylon to rise again and become the world's most cosmopolitan city before the second coming (but not necessarily before the rapture).

Incidentally, the description of last-days Babylon is one reason I foresee the demise of Islam. At the buckle of the Islamic "Koran Belt," Muslim leaders will not allow the construction of a sensuous manifestation of greed, which Babylon will become. Western materialism is anathema to Islam. This bankrupt religion, however, will soon fall. It will leave in its place a spiritual vacuum, and the residents of the Muslim world—spiritually, educationally, and physically oppressed for hundreds of years—will go "hog wild" in building the world's most glitz-filled and flesh-revealed city.

A final prophecy for Babylon that we need to study before we see its relation to the Antichrist is the prediction of its destruction.

Both Jeremiah 50 and Revelation 17 predict the destruction of the literal, last-days city of Babylon. Jeremiah tells us that this destruction will come "from the land of the north" and that the city will become "plunder." He further enlightens us that this destruction is God's judgment, a repayment for Babylon's treatment of the Jews (Jer. 50:17-18) and as punishment for the cities arrogant founder, Nimrod (Jer. 50:24).

Some argue that the Jeremiah destruction has already taken place, but the details just do not fit. Babylon is to be destroyed, "'As when God overthrew Sodom and Gomorrah with its neighbors,' declares the LORD, 'No man will live there, nor will any son of man reside in it'" (Jer. 50:40). Further descriptions show Babylon as an utter ruin. While the ruins of Babylon have certainly been drastic, there are records of men residing there through the centuries, and even today there are bricks in place from ancient Babylon. One of Saddam Hussein's largest projects was rebuilding the ancient city as a monument to his greatness.

Rebel to the End

So if Babylon will rise again to become a great city, only to be utterly destroyed, who is its destroyer?

Remember that Jeremiah said Babylon would be destroyed "from the land of the north." Remember also that the "little horn" of Daniel and Isaiah was the king of the North! I believe the Bible teaches that the Antichrist himself destroys Babylon in a fit of rage.

Why would he destroy a city of sensuality and greed? It is likely even a city the Antichrist himself has built.

Revelation 17 gives the answer, but first we must see Revelation 14:8: "And another angel, a second one, followed, saying, 'Fallen, fallen is Babylon the great, she who has made all the nations drink of the wine of the passion of her immorality.'"

Many theologians say that this verse, placed shortly after the midpoint of the tribulation, is a glimpse of things to come, a "fast-forward" and a foreshadow, and that it does not take place in the context of Revelation 14. I do not agree; I believe that Revelation 17–18 are the full description of what takes place in Revelation 14:8. The tribulation ends at the end of Revelation 16. Chronologically chapter 19 follows chapter 16. This explains why the battle of Armageddon is at the conclusion of chapter 16 but seems to take place *before* the fall of Babylon.

Many also view the Babylon of Revelation 17–18 as two different cities, one symbolic (17) and one literal (18). I do not see ample evidence to take chapter 17 as symbolic and rather see them as one description of a single destruction.

Babylon falls chronologically somewhere in the second half of the tribulation, chronologically in Revelation 14. So how does Babylon fall at the hands of the Antichrist? Follow with me through

Revelation 17 for the unveiling of the final rebellion of Babylon.

In verse 1 we are told that we are about to see the judgment of "the great harlot." More about this title later, but it should immediately give some indication of character. This harlot "sits on many waters," and verse 15 tells us that these waters are "peoples and multitudes and nations and tongues." In verse 3 we see this same harlot called "a woman sitting on a scarlet beast." In both of these descriptions, "sitting on" does not describe power and control but dependence and union. Babylon is dependent on the nations of the world as well as the scarlet beast. This beast has ten horns and is the Antichrist (made clear by verse 8).

In verse 16 an interesting turn takes place. The beast and his followers turn to *hate the harlot* and *make her desolate* and *will eat her flesh and will burn her up with fire*. Why do they do this? "For God has put it in their hearts to execute His purpose by having a common purpose, and by giving their kingdom to the beast, until the words of God will be fulfilled" (Rev. 17:17).

Let that sink in for a moment. God works in the heart of the Antichrist so that he has a *common purpose* and destroys Babylon so that *the words of God will be fulfilled*. Which words? The words of destruction found in Jeremiah 50!

Revelation 18 gives more insight. The early verses rejoice in the fallen condition of Babylon, much like Revelation 14:8. Compare and contrast Revelation 14:8 with Revelation 18:2-3.

And another angel, a second one, followed, saying, "Fallen, fallen is Babylon the great, she who has made all the nations drink of the wine of the passion of her immorality." (Rev. 14:8)

And he cried out with a mighty voice, saying, "Fallen, fallen is Babylon the great! . . . For all the nations have drunk of the wine of the passion of her immorality, and the kings of the earth have committed acts of immorality with her, and the merchants of the earth have become rich by the wealth of her sensuality." (Rev. 18:2-3)

Clearly these are the same events, taking place in the context of Revelation 14:8.

The key to the two chapters is Revelation 17:16: "And the ten horns which you saw, and the beast, these will hate the harlot and will make her desolate and naked, and will eat her flesh and will burn her up with fire."

The Antichrist himself will destroy Babylon. That the Babylon spoken of is *not* symbolic is made clear by Revelation 17:18, which reveals that "the woman" is "the great city." Further evidence is found in Revelation 18:4-5 where Jewish people are told to "come out of her" because "her sins have piled up as high as heaven," echoing the words of

Jeremiah 51:6-9 (among others), a passage that is clearly speaking of the literal city of Babylon.

So the scenario given in Revelation is that the Antichrist rebuilds the city of Babylon as an icon of humanism, but humanism always runs amok. As the Antichrist takes his place as God, his own city of Babylon does not comply, having become too secular to have a taste for religion. This so infuriates the Antichrist that he and his faithful followers will "hate the harlot," now an appropriate name for one who has turned away from her original commitment toward the Antichrist. In the greatest military movement of shock and awe the world has seen to that point, the Antichrist will bring down the city of Babylon in a single hour, fulfilling the centuries-old prophecies of the desolation of Babylon given by Jeremiah (Jeremiah 50–51).

Chapter 10

Consolidating
Worldwide Power

Along with destroying the city of Babylon in order to consolidate his power, the Antichrist will use his miraculous powers, his death and resurrection, and a strict control of the world economy to bring him to full control of all the world's political and financial powers.

Wonder-Working Power

Our world is amazed with miracles. Even the slightest hint of the miraculous will draw unbelievable attention and unmanageable crowds. Apparitions of Mary or bleeding statues of Jesus will draw throngs of hopeful followers. Charlatan evangelists offering miraculous cures will fill stadiums with large crowds of people with many needing a miracle. This world loves miracles!

The Bible says that the Antichrist will use miraculous power to draw crowds to himself.

Jesus says that "false Christs" will arise in the end days and "will show great signs and wonders." These signs and wonders will be so powerful that they would "mislead, if possible, even the elect" (Matt. 24:24).

Paul narrows "false Christs" to the Antichrist himself when he speaks of "the one whose coming is in accord with the activity to Satan, with all power and signs and false wonders" (2 Thess. 2:9). John reveals further that the Antichrist uses these signs and wonders to deceive "those who dwell on the earth" (Rev. 13:14). In the end, at the Battle of Armageddon, the demonic powers of signs and wonders draw together the kings of the earth to prepare for the great battle (Rev. 16:13-14).

In today's magic shows, we know that slight of hand and illusion are behind the acts. In the magic of the Antichrist, Satan will be behind it all. We have already read that the Antichrist comes "in accord with the activity of Satan" (2 Thess. 2:9), and Revelation 13:2 says further that "the dragon gave him his power."

But are these true miracles or the illusion of the miraculous?

To understand, let's look at six words for *miracles* that could have been used in the Greek language.

Wonders—This word almost always has a reference to divine acts that instill amazement in the minds of those who see them.

Mighty Deeds—Often translated "miracles" (as in Matt. 11:20), the word carries the connotation of power. The Greek word is

143

a derivative of the same word from which we get *dynamite*, *dynamic*, and *dynasty*, all words that have a connection with power. In the Bible it is always a word used of miraculous power.

Works—This word sometimes includes miracles ("the *works* of Christ") but most often is a summary word of works both miraculous and mundane.

Signs—Used seventy-eight times in the New Testament, this is the most prolific of the "miracle" words. It carries greater strength than a sign of information, signifying actions that are prominent and visible and display divine power. The term is often used with the word *wonders* and displays the fact that miracles *point to* something and are not just a display of power for power's sake.

Magic—This word always has a negative tone connected with witchcraft, such as with Simon, who was "astonishing the people of Samaria, claiming to be someone great" in Acts 8:9.

Sorceries—Also used negatively with the connotation of demonic activity, this word is never used of God's miracles.

The terms *magic* and *sorceries* are never divine. When the New Testament begins to describe the works of the Antichrist, it uses the miraculous words of wonders, mighty deeds, and signs, not the "illusion" words of magic or sorcery. While some want to deny the miracle-working power of the Antichrist, the grammar of the Bible just does not support such a denial.

Two miracles are impossible to deal with for those who want to deny the real miracles of the Antichrist. Revelation 13:13 says that the Antichrist "even makes fire come down out of heaven to the earth in the presence of men." To deny this as a real miracle, one would also have to deny that Elijah's experience was real. Also in Revelation 13 we are taught that the Antichrist gives "breath to the image of the beast" to make it "come to life" so that it "would even speak."

His greatest miracle, however, is what causes many to accept him as Messiah.

Raised from the Dead

Though we are not given any detail, we are told that the Antichrist will receive a "fatal wound" (Rev. 13:3). In spite of this wound of death, however, the Antichrist is healed and rises again. This causes "the whole earth" to follow the Antichrist.

Some skeptics want to say that this is a wound from which he *should* have died but did not.

On March 30, 1981, newly inaugurated President Ronald Reagan was shot outside the Washington

Hilton Hotel in Washington, DC. We know now that Reagan barely escaped with his life. It was a wound from which he *should have* died. American's responded in a proper manner, grateful to God that his life was spared. We were not so amazed, however, that we began to follow him as if he were a god. This is because many people sustain wounds from which they *should have* died but did not. This is grace for which we are thankful, but it is not the kind of miracle that causes the entire world to take note.

Will the Antichrist die from this fatal wound, or is it just that he should die?

Consider the language. It is the same language used of Christ, who is referred to by John as "a Lamb standing, as if slain" (Rev. 5:6). The "as if" clause is the same used of the Antichrist by the same author who writes, "I saw one of his heads as if it had been slain" (Rev. 13:3). We have no grammatical claim to say that the "as if" for Christ was an actuality but the "as if" for the Antichrist was a close call. Indeed, many liberal theologians claim that Christ "swooned" and only appeared "as if" He died. This is Christian heresy. If we defend the actual death of Christ, we must defend the actual death of the Antichrist. "As if" is used as the comparative image, not the potential image. The Greek word translated "as if" has no hint of potentiality, only comparison.

Further, when Jesus was raised from the dead, Peter rushed into the tomb and, seeing just the linen wrappings, "went away to his home, marveling" (Luke 24:12). Later that evening when Jesus appeared in the upper room, the disciples could not believe it was Him because of their "amazement" (Luke 24:41). John used the same words "marvel" and "amazed" when he described the world's response to the resurrection of the Antichrist (see Rev. 13:3; 17:8). The world's response, after amazement, will be to say, "Who is like the beast?" and then they begin to follow him fully.

Some question whether Satan has the power to raise the dead. Any negative answers in this arena are *assumed* answers, not *revealed* answers. Further, since the Antichrist is working at the bidding of God, who is to say that God is not the one who will raise him?

This death and resurrection of the Antichrist happens during the middle years of the tribulation, before the "abomination of desecration" and the fall of Babylon.

Spiritual Control

After being raised from the dead and destroying "the harlot" Babylon, the Antichrist consolidates political control. The next item on the agenda is to consolidate religious control (these do not necessarily take place in this order). After his death and resurrection, the prophet of the Antichrist will make "the earth and those who dwell in it to worship the first beast" (Rev. 13:12).

How will he *make* the earth worship him? I believe he will use demon-possessed idols. We are told that the whole earth will be forced to worship the beast and that this worship will be directed toward "an image of the beast" (Rev. 13:14); those who "do not worship the image of the beast" will be killed (Rev. 13:15).

To give some support for this demon-possessed idol theory, let me show you what *seems* to be a contradiction. If all the earth is to worship the image of the beast, then why do both Revelation 9:20 and Isaiah 2:17-20 indicate that some remain who do not "repent of the works of their hands, so as not to worship demons, and the idols of gold" (Rev. 9:20). Both passages use the plural, *idols*. If the Antichrist gains complete devotion, why do some remain who worship *idols* rather than his image?

The answer is right before us and brings a chilling revelation. Revelation 13:14 says that the Antichrist tells "those who dwell on the earth to make an image of the beast." Our minds always assume that this is *one* image when, in fact, the instruction is that every person is to make "an image." The singular is used because it is connected with single individuals, not because there is a single image. The same grammar is used in Revelation 13:16 where everyone is forced to be given "a mark." This mark—singular—is actually millions of marks—plural.

Now that everyone has made (or presumably purchased or otherwise attained) an image of the beast, the Antichrist, with the devil's power, gives "breath" to each individual image. That is, each individual idol becomes demon possessed to become the great monitoring system to know *who* is worshipping and *who* is not. The images literally take on a life of their own. "And it was given to him to give breath to the image of the beast, so that the image of the beast would even speak and cause as many as do not worship the image of the beast to be killed" (Rev. 13:15).

Who will succumb to this pressure to worship the demon-possessed images of the beast? As in the days of Nebuchadnezzar, there will only be a few will *not* succumb.

Many of the unredeemed members of apostate churches will succumb. "But the Spirit explicitly says that in later times some will fall away from the faith, paying attention to deceitful spirits and doctrines of demons" (1 Tim. 4:1).

Many unbelieving Jews will succumb.

They will fling their silver into the streets and their gold will become an abhorrent thing; their silver and their gold will not be able to deliver them in the day of the wrath of the LORD. They cannot satisfy their appetite nor can they fill their stomachs, for their iniquity has become an occasion of stumbling. They transformed the beauty of His ornaments into pride, and they made the images of their abominations and their detestable things with it; therefore I will make it an abhorrent thing to them (Ezek. 7:19-20).

Notice that in this passage, the images they made with their own hands (turning their silver and gold into images of the beast) will become "an abhorrent thing to them." This is a message of hope, that many Jews will see their folly in trusting in the Antichrist. When the one behind the image becomes a modern-day Hitler, many Jews will flee from the Antichrist and will be received by the real Christ!

Economic Control

Now controlling the political and religious worlds, the Antichrist will make his final move of power when he seizes complete control of the world's economy, on both a macro and a micro level.

The manner of executing complete economic control is the required mark, the infamous 666. Those without the mark are unable to participate in the economic markets of the world, either buying or selling.

Some believe that trying to discern this meaning is futile, and it certainly can be. J. H. Strong said that efforts to discern its meaning is "the basis of much vain speculation."

While it can be, we also read in Revelation 13:18 that we are instructed to discern the meaning of the mark and its number. "Here is wisdom. Let him who has understanding calculate the number of the beast, for the number is that of a man; and his number is six hundred and sixty-six" (Rev. 13:18).

The word *calculate* is given in the imperative; that is, it is a command! It is a math word that is related to the Greek word for "pebble." In the ancient world stones would be used to keep track of count. From this, stones began to take the transferred sense of reaching a verdict. In Revelation 2:17 the church at Pergamum will receive a white stone, indicating the "verdict" or "calculation" of innocence.

To calculate this number is not an easy task! Do a little research, and you will see that every odd estimation of meaning has been given.

The *Theological Dictionary of the New Testament (Abridged)*, in its discussion of the Greek word behind "calculate" says one interpretation is that 666 is the sum of the numbers 1 to 36, and that 36 is the sum of the numbers 1–8, and that in Greek Gnosticism (popular in John's day), the number 8 was equivalent to *Sophia*, the goddess of wisdom, and thus 666 was a reference to Gnosticism! (Interestingly, the Antichrist *is* described as the eighth ruler in Revelation 17:11). Others use equally fanciful calculations to determine that 666 refers to the Roman Emperor Domitian.[9] Some Seventh-day Adventists are reported to believe that "the mark of the beast" is to worship on Sunday rather than on Saturday!

As you calculate, take extreme caution. Any allegorical interpretation will get you in trouble. The number has a specific and calculable answer which, I believe, will be obvious to those with discernment in the days of the reign of the Antichrist.

Possibly the meaning is wrapped up in *gematria*, the ancient system of connecting number values to letters of the alphabet. Converting English letters to Greek, my name adds to 939. Bill Clinton is 602. Closer, but still not the Antichrist!

Jesus, interestingly, adds to 888. The number six is the number for man, seven is for perfection, and eight is the number for "beyond perfection." It is often said that Jesus arose on the eighth day (one day after the seventh—calling the Sabbath the eighth day relates to the Feast of the Tabernacles, which is a seven-day feast followed by a day of rejoicing). Circumcision was performed on the eighth day. Biblical numerologists such as E. W. Bullinger have written extensively on the values of both six and eight, as well as other significant Bible numbers.

I do not believe that the number refers to someone in the past but rather in the future. When the time comes, those with spiritual discernment will be able to see it clearly.

Are you a believer? If so, you really do not need to spend inordinate amounts of time calculating this number. The instruction was written to those who will be living in the days of the Antichrist. Today's believers will be snatched out of this world through rapture. For those who may be reading these words *after* the rapture, I pray that this book has been found to be accurate to the Word of God, the standard by which you should judge them. I encourage you to follow God's instruction and seek how to "calculate the number of the beast."

Now the Antichrist has consolidated political, religious, and economic control. Where does the world go next?

Chapter 11

Darkness and Doom

The closing days of the reign of the Antichrist will bring some of the most dreadful events in history. These will be days of unrivaled wickedness and suffering. Daniel predicts "a time of distress such as never occurred since there was a nation" (Dan. 12:1). Jesus said that "unless the Lord had shortened those days, no life would have been saved." (Mark 13:19-20).

Why would a good God allow such wanton destruction and such ravaging heartache? In actuality, God not only permits it but in these last days He authorizes it. Those who do not believe that God causes destruction have failed to read the history of Israel!

The purpose of these days of destruction is for God to avenge the world's attitude and action against His Word. To neglect the Word of God is serious business. First, God avenges the world's attitude and actions toward His Word in the flesh, Jesus Christ. In the final days of the Antichrist, God avenges the murder of His Son. But He also avenges the attitudes and action toward His Word in print as He pours out his wrath against those who trampled the truth of Holy Scripture. Paul teaches that the Antichrist will come "with all power and signs and false wonders" and his wickedness and work will be "because they did not receive the love of the truth so as to be saved" (2 Thess. 2:10). Just two verses later Paul reiterates that these dark days are for the judgment of those "who did not believe the truth, but took pleasure in wickedness" (2 Thess. 2:12).

God always uses an instrument of destruction. It was Assyria for Israel, Babylon for Judah. Isaiah proclaimed, "Woe to Assyria, the rod of My anger and the staff in whose hands is My indignation" (Isa. 10:5). Assyria was "the rod" of God's anger and "the staff" of His indignation, but the ultimate woe came not to Israel, whom God destroyed, but to Assyria through whom God destroyed. Incidentally, when the Bible talks of God's rod and staff, it is not always in a comforting, pastoral scene!

The instrument of destruction God will use in the end is the Antichrist himself. As God's tool, the Antichrist will receive unbelievable power and freedom from God. But even with the Antichrist's long leash, it does come to an end. God has set our limitations.

Let me take you through a play-by-play of the last events on earth.

The Abomination of Desolation

One of the most well-known aspects of the great tribulation (though often misunderstood) is the abomination of desolation. Jesus referred to it, and the prophet Daniel wrote about it. This seemingly high point of the Antichrist's career is the mark of the beginning of his doom. It is the point at which the Antichrist has garnered full control of political and economic resources and now seals the deal on spiritual resources of this world. His victory is displayed as he exalts and magnifies himself and begins to speak "monstrous things" against our God.

Daniel 11:36 says that when he does this, he will "prosper." There can only be two reasons why prosperity would come to the one who speaks monstrous things of Almighty God. First, in those days mankind will be so far from God that the Antichrist will, in reality, be speaking the words of the people. The consummate politician, this man will speak the mind that has become the people of the last days. Micah the prophet spoke of days in which "if a man walking after wind and falsehood has told lies. . . . he would be the spokesman to this people" (Mic. 2:11). When the Antichrist speaks monstrous things against God and His Son, the people of that age will arise and say a hearty "amen!"

A second reason the Antichrist prospers is simply because God allows it. The word Daniel uses for "prosper" is found eighty-one times in Scripture, and in an overwhelming number of verses the connection is with the prosperity from the Lord. We see this twice in the life of Joseph, first under Potiphar and then under the jailer, where we are told the Lord caused all Joseph did to *prosper* (Gen. 39:3, 23). Dozens of times the word is used in connection with the hand of the Lord. This gives every indication that prosperity, even for the Antichrist, comes only with the authorization of God.

And, indeed, God's authorization for the Antichrist's prosperity does come to an end. At its peak with garnering of spiritual power, he prospers "until the indignation is finished" (Dan. 11:36).

The indignation is the work of God, His anger and wrath. The term *indignation* is often used as the name for the tribulation by Old Testament writers.

The prosperity of the Antichrist is only an instrument through which God works His indignation. After God has successfully expressed His wrath, the prosperity of the Antichrist will cease.

The abomination of desolation comes with a great warning for Jewish people. Isaiah the prophet warned that "until the indignation runs its course" God's people, the Jews, should "enter into your rooms, close your doors behind you; hide for a little while. . . . For behold, the Lord is about to come out from His place to punish the inhabitants of the earth for their iniquity; and the earth will reveal her bloodshed and will no longer cover her slain" (Isa. 26:20). Jesus makes the case for hiding even stronger, saying that when the abomination comes, Jews should "flee to the mountains" with no going back to gather even basic supplies (Matt. 24:15-18).

The abomination of desolation is the act of Antichrist declaring himself to be God. Daniel 11:37 shows the extent of the Antichrist's rejection of the faiths of this world:

- "He will show no regard for the gods of his fathers" —a rejection of Judaism.

- "He will show no regard . . . for the desire of women"—a rejection of Christianity. Using this passage, some incorrectly teach that the Antichrist is homosexual. The "desire of women," however, is a noun, not a verb. The passage does not say that he has no regard for the passion (verb) of women, but for that which women desire. And what was it that women in Daniel's day would desire? The desire of every Jewish woman was to be the mother of the promised "seed of a woman" from Genesis 3:15! The desire of women, therefore, is the Messiah! This is why, upon the announcement to Mary by Gabriel, she rejoiced that God "has had regard for the humble state of His bond-slave; for behold, from this time on all genera-tions will count me blessed" (Luke 1:48).

- "Nor will he show regard for any other god"—the rejection of all religious faith save that in himself.

After the abomination of desolation on earth, a cosmic battle takes place in heaven.

The War in Heaven

Revelation 12:7-12 tells about a coming "war in heaven" where Michael and his angels wage war with the dragon. During this war Satan is cast from heaven once for all. With this victory a loud voice proclaims, "Now the salvation, and the power, and the kingdom of our God and the authority of His Christ have come, for the accuser of our brethren has been thrown down." As blessed as this event is, a "woe" given to the earth and sea "because the devil has come down to you, having great wrath, knowing that he has only a short time." This short time is literally hell on earth.

Both Revelation and Daniel tell us that the angel Michael has a major role in this battle. Daniel's word is small, but we are told that before the "time of distress such as never occurred since there was a nation," that "Michael, the great prince who stands guard, . . . will arise" (Dan. 12:1). Michael is shown to be the head of heaven's armies, the guardian angel of Israel, the one who gives the shout of return at the rapture, and the archangel of all the angelic host.

While many view this war in heaven as a flashback to the original fall of Lucifer, I believe John is referring to a future event. Currently Satan remains as the "accuser of the brethren," as seen so vividly in the book of Job. Revelation pictures Satan as one "who deceives the whole world" and will be cast from heaven. These two aspects of Satan's current reign make it impossible that John's account of war would be a past event.

So Satan is in heaven today? No! However, today Satan does have access to heaven. In a manner in which we are not fully aware, Satan is able to attain access to God in order to accuse the brethren. God allows this because it fits within His divine decree of Satan's lot. On the day that Satan looses this access, he will know that his time is limited and that he has lost the war. At this future time the heavens and those who dwell in them will rejoice, but the earth and the sea will be recipients of his great anger.

The Final Pogrom

Now that the Antichrist has established himself as god, and Satan has been angered by banishment from access to God, the final pogrom toward the elimination of the Jews begins in earnest. Every Jew and all things Jewish become the intense focus of the government of the Antichrist, with a desire toward elimination. In Hitler only a glimpse of Jewish hatred was seen.

The prophet Amos speaks of these days. His words are often used of our day, but we have only a foretaste of the barrenness of faith that is coming to the world. Amos says that the day will come when God sends a famine for "hearing the words of the Lord." In that day the citizens of the earth will "stagger from sea to sea" and they will go to and fro looking and longing for a word from God, "but they will not find it." These days will be accompanied by great distress and turmoil, it will be a day in which every song is a lamentation, and every joy turns to bitterness. It will be "like a time of mourning for an only son." (Amos 8:12).

While all the peoples of the world will suffer, no group will be more chastised and ostracized than the Jews. Satan has always had a fury against the Jews because they represent for him the sovereign purpose of God that thwarts his own schemes. He knows that through the Jewish people all the world will be blessed through God's Son. If Satan can destroy the Jewish people, he will take every opportunity.

I believe Psalm 74 was written in advance as the song of the Jews during these future days. Every word of this Psalm not only gives insight into the activity of that day but, more painfully, gives insight into the brokenhearted cry of the Jew of that day. Take time to read the entire psalm but consider especially these words:

- Why have you rejected us forever?

- Remember your congregation!

- Remember Mount Zion where You have dwelt. . . . The enemy has damaged everything within the sanctuary.

- They have burned all the meeting places of God in the land.

- There is no longer any prophet, nor is there any among us who knows how long.

- Will the enemy spurn Your name forever?

The final days bring on horrible difficulty for the world, but the Jews receive the horror of horrors and the worst of the worst.

Jewish Cries Arise

The cries of the Jewish people will rise. They will fall on the deaf ears of politicians, the business community, and Gentile friends and neighbors. God, however, listens! The Lord, we are told through the prophet Zechariah, takes special concern when a Jew is mistreated. God said that the one who touches the Jew, "touches the apple of His eye." After the time of cleansing that draws Jews to God (the vast majority of Jews today are non-practicing secularists), Jesus Christ will come forth, sent by the Father in answer to the prayers of Jews. Because the Antichrist has led the world to plunder the Jews, the Lord of hosts says, "After glory He has sent Me against the nations." The Jews will cry to Jesus, and He will rescue them!

Isaiah 10 has a double application of the past: Israel and its destruction by the Assyrians and of the future days of tribulation when the Antichrist (an Assyrian Jew) will seek again to destroy Israel. In this chapter Jews are told, "Do not fear the Assyrian who strikes you" because "in a very little while My indignation against you will be spent." When God's wrath has fully cleansed Israel, God's anger will be redirected from the Jews through the Assyrian and his armies, and the anger of the Lord will then "be directed to their destruction."

Just as God heard the cries of the Jewish people in Exodus, His ear will be attentive to the cries of Jews in the days of the tribulation, and He will answer!

Rebellion in Egypt and the Trampling of Israel

The Lord gives, and the Lord takes away. God had allowed the Antichrist to enjoy prosperity and success even while he was eradicating the Christian faith and the Jewish people from the earth. God used this to allow His wrath to be executed. But every leash comes to its end.

Isaiah the prophet says that when the time comes, "the Lord of hosts will arouse a scourge against him" (Isa. 10:26). Daniel gives great insight into this "scourge" in Daniel 11:40-41. In these verses we learn that the king of the South will collide with the king of the North. Most likely this is a political collision, as the king of Egypt attempts to disagree with the king of the North—the Antichrist. This collision is met with swift retribution and military response, with the Antichrist storming against Egypt and trampling down any country that stands in his path. This resistance from Egypt is a stinging whip in the immeasurable ego of the Antichrist, and he will take all measures to ensure his own domestic tranquility.

One of the countries on the way to Egypt from Assyria is Israel. Daniel tells us that the Antichrist will enter "the Beautiful Land" and that, what is left of it, will be greatly damaged by the trampling of soldiers. Other nations (both on the path to Egypt and in collusion with Egypt) will be destroyed as the Antichrist bristles from the sting of this whip. However, as countries fall, three are rescued from the Antichrist's wrath: Edom, Moab, and Ammon.

Why are these three nations spared? Scripture offers the answer: they are spared because they are working *with* the Antichrist. Psalm 83 is a psalm of prophecy; there is no historical record of its fulfillment. It speaks of the nations of the world coming together in a scheme to wipe Israel off the map (Iran's Ahmadinijad was vocal but not very original in his agenda). Their desire will be, "that the name of Israel be remembered no more." Of the ten countries that covenant together to wipe Israel off the map, Edom, Moab, and Ammon are included (modern-day Jordan). Later these regions will regret their alliance. Balaam prophesied of a day when "a scepter shall rise from Israel and shall crush through the forehead of Moab, and . . . Edom shall be a possession" (Num. 24:17-18). This prophecy is again recited, with the inclusion of Ammon, in Isaiah 11:14 where it is revealed that Israel, after the tribulation, will "possess Edom and Moab, and the sons of Ammon will be subject to them."

Daniel 11:42-43 tells us that Egypt does not last long in its uprising, and with the fall of Egypt, Ethiopia and Libya quickly fall in line. North Africa is back under control. But now ... new rumors abound.

The Destruction of Babylon

As quickly as the Antichrist regains control of Egypt, Daniel says that "rumors from the East and from the North will disturb him" (Dan. 11:44). What are these troubled tidings? They are rumblings of rebellion in Babylon.

How does a cheated spouse normally first hear of the unfaithfulness of his or her mate? Typically rumor! As we discussed in chapter 9, Babylon begins to spread her wings, and the Antichrist is not amused. In fact, he responds to this infidelity with "great wrath" and goes on a rampage to "destroy and anni-hilate." Revelation 17:16 further describes the anni-hilation, when the beast and those with him "hate the harlot [Babylon] and will make her desolate and naked, and will eat her flesh and will burn her up with fire."

The days of peace brought on in the early rise of the Antichrist are short-lived. Just over three years into his reign, and he is having to "secure" this peace by crushing rebellion first in Egypt and then with greater fury in Babylon.

And now, with the taste of blood and the readi-ness for battle, the ultimate battleground comes into focus.

The Battle of Armageddon

The prophet Joel is told to proclaim to the nations, "Prepare a war!" And indeed, the nations prepare for war. Multitudes twice over gather in "the valley of decision." All implements of peace are retooled into

175

instruments of war. Even weak men are called to arms for the great battle. This call comes forth from the Lord, for the wine press is full and God has had enough (Joel 3).

While the battle cry goes out to the people to prepare for war, the spirits of demons go out to the kings of the world, gathering them for "the great day of God" (Rev. 16:14). As this day approaches, the citizens of the world should know that the Lord is coming quickly!

The nations begin to gather for war in "the valley of decision," which is the Valley of Armageddon. This valley, a swath of the most productive agricultural land on Earth, located in northern Israel, is the site of major battles from the judges, the kings of Israel, to World War I when General Allenby sealed the final days of the Ottoman Empire at the Battle of Megiddo. Napoleon is said to have marveled that all the armies of the world could gather in this vast plain. Easily more than two hundred battles have been fought in this vast plain.

When the preparation for the Battle of Armageddon begins, what happens to any Jews who may remain in Jerusalem? They are told to leave the city and flee, of all places, to Babylon! "There you will be rescued; there the LORD will redeem you from the hand of your enemies." This takes place when "many nations have been assembled against you" (Mic. 4:10-11). Why would Jews be told to flee to Babylon—the perennial enemy of all things Jewish? Babylon has become a safe hiding place because it has become a desolate place (Jer. 51). The Jews run in the direction of Babylon as the battle draws near. Perhaps John had this in view when it was revealed that "the two wings of the great eagle were given to the woman, so that she could fly into the wilderness to her place, where she was nourished" (Rev. 12:14). While there are likely other hiding places to which this refers, it is possible that Babylon becomes the ultimate place of refuge.

As the Antichrist comes as the commander in chief, he will set his command station "between the seas and the beautiful Holy Mountain" (Dan. 11:45)—thus to the west of the Holy City. Isaiah says, "He will halt at Nob" and shake "his fist at the mountain of the daughter of Zion, the hill of Jerusalem" (Isa. 10:32).

There are two common errors in thinking about the battle. One is that it takes place at Armageddon, and the second is that it is a battle! The Battle of Armageddon is not a battle, nor does it take place in Armageddon! As we will see, what really takes place is the preparation for a battle (which never comes) and the staging ground for the battle is the valley of Armageddon, with its vast spaces perfect for the gathering of large armies.

So where is Nob, the stopping place of the Antichrist? While there is no definitive answer that precisely locates ancient Nob, all agree that it is somewhere at the outskirts of Jerusalem. Many scholars claim that modern Mount Scopus, home to the Hebrew University, is the location of Nob. If this is true, the Antichrist will have a perfect stopping ground to overlook the city of Jerusalem and "shake his fist" at Mount Zion.

And soon he will march his armies down Mount Scopus and into the heart of ancient Jerusalem. Zechariah reveals that "the city will be captured, the houses plundered, the women ravished and half of the city exiled" (Zech. 14:2). The psalmist reveals that the kings of the earth will look toward Jerusalem, and the Jews and shout, "Let us tear their fetters apart and cast away their cords from us!" (Ps. 2:2-3).

But as soon as the battle ensues, the grand finale begins! As the Antichrist begins to capture the city, the heavens open, and a white horse and Victorious Warrior descend. On the horse is One called "faithful and true," and He begins to wage war. In close proximity to the Warrior, whose eyes are a flame of fire, are His armies, clothed in white linens and following Him on white horses. Zechariah says that, when this Warrior arrives, he will "go forth and fight against those nations, as when He fights on a day of battle" (Zech. 14:3). The Christ of God and the false Christ of Satan meet in confrontation, and Satan's incarnation loses in an instant.

The Bible records the ignominious deaths of many—death through slaughter, suicide, or sword. Some have their blood licked up by dogs; some are hanged on their own gallows; one is eaten by worms. But an unequaled fate concludes the career of the Man of Sin, who is instantly seized by the King of kings and Lord of lords, and this beast is cast into the Lake of Fire where he gains his eternal punishment.

Scripture is clear about the doom of the Antichrist. While he may prosper for a time, his doom is sure. Rejoice in the unequaled proclamation of the doom of the Antichrist:

- "He will be broken without human agency" (Dan. 8:25).

- "He will come to his end, and no one will help him" (Dan. 11:45).

- "The Lord will slay [the Lawless one] with the breath of His mouth and bring to an end by the appearance of His coming" (2 Thess. 2:8).

- "[He will] be thrown alive into the lake of fire which burns with brimstone" (Rev. 19:20).

- "[He] will be tormented day and night forever and ever" (Rev. 20:10).

The Final Destruction

As the followers of the Antichrist watch his destruction, they will meet an almost instant fate as well. Zechariah says that they will seize one another, go to war with one another, and then be destroyed in humiliation as "their flesh will rot while they stand on their feet, and their eyes will rot in their sockets, and their tongue will rot in their mouth" (Zech. 14:12-13). Both Old and New Testaments tell us that the remains of Antichrist's followers will be eaten by the birds.

With the Antichrist and his followers defeated and destroyed, the Lord will gather the nations before Him and judge them, separating the sheep from the goats. One criterion that will be used will be their treatment of Israel: "To the extent that you did it to one of these brothers of Mine, even the least of them, you did it to Me" (Matt. 25:40).

Satan will be bound for a thousand years, which shall be a millennium of peace, prosperity, and the fulfillment of God's original design for His creation. The nations will not be deceived, and Christ will reign as King on the restored throne of David. All the promises of God to Israel will be fulfilled during this coming day.

And the two-thousand-year-old prayer will be answered:

"Thy Kingdom Come!"

Acknowledgements

This project has been the result of a great amount of study over a period of several years. I am grateful to authors like A. W. Pink who wrote an exhaustive work on the Antichrist. Pink and others inspired me to search the Scriptures more deeply for God's revealed truth about the Antichrist.

My able editor, Judi Hayes, has made this work far more readable. Judi gave me my first break into writing fifteen years ago. Her passion for the written word that expresses the revealed truth is an inspiration. Her help on this project has been a gift from God.

Two of the churches I have had the privilege of serving as pastor have helped in this project. These truths first came out of study for a Wednesday night Pastor's Bible Study at First Baptist Church of Katy, Texas. My faithful Wednesday crowd was always a delight to teach, and their hungry minds spurred me to dive deeper into the truths of God's Word. The First Baptist Church of Munday, Texas (where I had the deep honor of beginning my pastoral ministry) allowed me to teach the finished product in a seminar format. Such teaching improved this final work.

I have a deep sense of gratitude to so many church members and Christian friends who have continually asked me how this project was progressing. Their unending desire to see the final project kept me going to the end!

I also want to share a word of gratitude to two young theologians who sharpened this work by reading the pre-publication draft. Danny Kirkpatrick is a Pastor and doctoral student. His theological and grammatical insights were fresh and accurate. Andrew Hebert is a graduate of Criswell College and a graduate student at Criswell. He is a sharp thinker and strong communicator. Both of these men challenged my assumptions and assertions, and their input into the final draft made this a much better work. I alone retain credit for the errors remaining!

And my wonderful wife, Shelley, and two children, Hannah and Nathan, allowed me many late nights at the laptop with the sometimes arduous task of putting one word after another to create a sentence, paragraph, chapter, and—eventually—a book!

I put this work into print with a fair degree of hesitation. Any work on prophecy is an inexact science! Should I someday be found wrong on my conclusions, I ask your forgiveness and grace. This is one pastor's attempt to "rightly divide the word of truth." By God's grace, it will be used to guide others in their personal quest to do the same.

Glossary

Abomination of Desolation—The biblical title used to describe the activity of the Antichrist when he sets himself up in the Jewish temple to be worshipped as God. Daniel 9:27 says, "And he [the Antichrist] will make a firm covenant with the many for one week, but in the middle of the week he will put a stop to sacrifice and grain offering; and on the wing of abominations will come one who makes desolate, even until a complete destruction, one that is decreed, is poured out on the one who makes desolate." Later, Daniel 11:31 says, "Forces from him [the Antichrist] will arise, desecrate the sanctuary fortress, and do away with the regular sacrifice. And they will set up the abomination of desolation." According to Daniel 12:11 this abomination takes place 1,290 days before the second coming. Jesus warns Jews that when they see the abomination of desolation, they should flee, without going back to gather their things (Matt. 24:15-18).

Antichrist—The term used to describe the coming world leader. He will lead the world in all realms: economic, political, and spiritual. Rising from obscurity, he will at first be hailed as a peacemaker. Many Jews will accept him as their long-awaited Messiah. The first distinguishing mark of his identity is the peace treaty he will sign with Israel, bringing long-awaited peace to the Middle East. Midway through this peace, however, he will set himself up as God and will begin the greatest time of persecution upon the Jews the world has ever seen.

Amillennial—the belief that the teachings about a coming thousand-year reign of Christ on Earth are to be taken in a spiritual manner rather than literally. This teaching places the rapture and the second coming together as a simultaneous event, immediately followed by the judgment and the eternal condition of heaven or hell.

The Beast—The term John uses for the Antichrist in the book of Revelation. John uses this term thirty-one times in the Revelation, always referring to the Antichrist.

Covenant of Peace—A distinguishing mark of the commencement of the seven-year period of tribulation and of the identity of the Antichrist. when the Antichrist makes a "firm covenant" with Israel for seven years (one week, or one "set of sevens" according to Daniel 9:27). When this covenant is signed, the final seven years of Daniel's prophetic timeclock for Israel and the world begins (Dan. 9:25-27).

Dispensational—A method of interpreting Scripture, especially prophecy, which divides history into several eras, or dispensations. A dispensationalist holds to a future role for the nation of Israel rather than a "replacement" theology that teaches that the church has replaced Israel. Dispensationalists believe that many errors in scriptural interpretation have been made because interpreters do not "rightly divide the word of truth" (2 Tim. 2:15). Dispensationalists are often criticized for believing in different manners of salvation in different dispensations, though this is not an accurate criticism. Dispensationalists teach that believers of all ages are saved by grace through faith.

The Dragon—A cryptic term referring to Satan used by John fourteen times in Revelation. Revelation 20:2 reveals the dragon as "the serpent of old, who is the devil and Satan."

Eschatology—The study of last things, or end times. Often a general term referring to the study of biblical prophecy.

Eternal state—The eternal time that begins after the close of the millennium. Also described as the new heaven and new Earth.

End Times—The last days of the history of man. "Latter days" refer to the time approaching the "last days," which are the days from the rapture of the church through the end of the millennium.

The Great Harlot—A descriptive reference to the last-days city of Babylon. Having been created by the Antichrist to serve his purposes, the city instead becomes unmanageable. Having turned from her creator, the city is seen as a harlot. In rage, the Antichrist destroys the harlot "in a single hour" (Revelation 18:10).

Humanism—A philosophy or worldview that holds that humans have within themselves the capacity for spiritual well-being without the need of a Savior.

Kingdom of God—A term often erroneously used to refer to any rule and reign of God (though this is better referred to as God's sovereignty). The kingdom of God is a major theme of both the Old and the New Testament, especially revealed in the Old Testament prophecies and taught by John the Baptist and the early ministry of Jesus Christ. In its strictest sense (and best usage), the kingdom of God begins when the Son of Man (Jesus Christ) is given the earthly throne of His Father, David, and "all the peoples, nations and men of every language might serve Him" (Dan. 7:14). This kingdom is closely connected with the covenants God made to Abraham and David.

Lake of Fire—A term used by John in Revelation to refer to eternal hell. It is the final destination of the Antichrist (Rev. 19:20), Satan (Rev. 20:10), and anyone whose "name was not found written in the book of life" (Rev. 20:15).

Little Horn—The description of the Antichrist used by Daniel. This horn is little in comparison with ten horns, which represent ten earthly kingdoms. The little horn is an eleventh, which rises small but becomes exceedingly large (Dan. 8:9).

Mahdi—The Mahdi is taught by Muslims to be a coming world leader who will restore justice and proper religion to the world. While many Christians teach that the Antichrist will be the Muslim Mahdi, I foresee the collapse of Islam and the rise of a non-Muslim end-time ruler who will be the Antichrist as taught in Scripture.

Marriage Supper of the Lamb—The banquet feast held in heaven with Christ and the raptured church, taking place after the rapture and before the second coming, during the days when the tribulation in concluding on Earth. In ancient Jewish custom the marriage supper takes place before the processional of the Groom with His bride. Revelation 19:9 says, "Blessed are those who are invited to the marriage supper of the Lamb."

Messianic Age—The age of the coming earthly reign of the Messiah. It will be a time of peace, prosperity, health, and the lordship of Jesus Christ. It is characterized by great peace when "the wolf will dwell with the lamb" (Isa. 11:6; 65:25). Jerusalem will be the capital city, and Jesus will reign from the restored throne of David. This age will last a thousand years (Rev. 20:1-6), and thus is also called the millennial kingdom.

Millennial Kingdom—See "Messianic Age."

Millennium—The thousand-year period of the messianic age. Revelation 20:1-6 describes the length, and many Old Testament passages refer to the content of this coming age. It is the fulfillment of the prayer, "Thy kingdom come."

Postmillennialism—An end-times worldview that believes the world will see continual improvement and the church will experience greater and greater victories as time progresses, eventually conquering sin and evil to a large degree. At the end of this period of betterment (taken either as a literal or figurative thousand years), Christ will return to Earth, and the final judgment will take place, leading into the eternal state.

Premillennial—The end-times worldview that believes the second coming of Christ will take place prior to the thousand years of peace described in Revelation 20:1-7. Premillennialists are often divided into two camps: dispensational and historical. The dispensational group believes that this current age will end with the rapture of the church, followed by seven years of tribulation and then the second coming, all before the thousand-year reign of Christ on Earth. The historical group generally does not believe in a pretribulational rapture of the church but believes Christians will endure the tribulation while on Earth.

Preterist—The interpretation of Scripture that believes events of the book of Revelation and other related prophecies have already been fulfilled in history.

Rapture—The belief that the church (Christians) will be raptured (or snatched out) of this world prior to the second coming of Christ. The word *rapture* comes from the Latin word meaning "snatched out" or "caught up" and is used in the Latin translation of 1 Thessalonians 4:17. Those who believe in the rapture believe that it is imminent (nothing remains to be fulfilled before the rapture can occur). They also believe it will take place so quickly that it is invisible to the human eye. Those who believe in a pretribulation rapture believe it will occur before the seven years of the tribulation. A smaller number believe in a mid-tribulation or post-tribulation rapture.

Second Coming—The return of Christ to Earth as recorded in Revelation 19:11-19. The second coming and the rapture are two separate and distinct events. Care must be taken to ensure that the two are not comingled when interpreting Scripture. In general, the second coming is visible while the rapture is invisible (or "in the twinkling of an eye"). The second coming happens at the end of the tribulation and prior to the millennial kingdom.

Tribulation—The period of time in which God's wrath is displayed on the Earth for the rejection of His Son. According to a literal translation of Daniel 9:27, this period is seven years in duration. During this time the Antichrist will rule the world in a one-world government and economy. Great ecological disasters will remodel the earth, preparing it for the millennial kingdom. God will use this time for punishment and to restore Israel to its covenantal position as the chosen nation of God through whom all the world will be blessed. The tribulation ends in the Battle of Armageddon and the second coming of Christ.

Endnotes

1 Henry Ernest Nichol, We've a Story to Tell to the Nations. Public Domain.

2 Francisco, Clyde T. *Broadman Bible commentary*. Revised ed. Vol. 1. Nashville: Broadman, 1973. 171.

3 Arthur Walkington Pink, *The Antichrist* (Swengel, PA: Bible Truth Depot, 1923; reprint with new foreword: Bellingham, WA: Logos Research Systems, 2005), 219.

4 "WeJew Jewish Video Sharing Megasite - Singer &Amp; Gimpel 07/30 Show 4 Pt II The Jewish Messiah." *The Jewish Messiah*. WeJew. Web. Dec. 2009. <http://wejew.com/media/5707/Singer_

_Gimpel_0730_Show_4_Pt_II_The_Jewish_
Messiah/>

5 "New Nations Guide FactMonster.com." *Fact
Monster:* "A Guide to New Nations," Web. Nov.
2009. <http://www.factmonster.com/spot/coun-
tries1.html.>.

6 "Ask the Rabbi - Am I Jewish? - Jewish
Identity." *About Judaism.* Web. <http://judaism.
about.com/library/3_askrabbi_o/bl_simmons_
amijewish.htm>.

7 *The Nimrod Restaurant.* Web. <http://www.then-
imrod.com>.

8 "NIMROD Vision Statement." *NIMROD Home
page.* Web. <https://nimrodteam.org/vision.
html>.

9 Gerhard Kittel, Gerhard Friedrich, and Geoffrey
William Bromiley, *Theological Dictionary of
the New Testament,* trans. of *Theologisches
Worterbuch Zum Neuen Testament* (Grand Rapids,
Mich.: W. B. Eerdmans, 1995, © 1985), 1342.

LaVergne, TN USA
12 March 2010
175804LV00002B/2/P